LOVE BEING A HUMAN

WAKING UP

by Shirley Battie

ISBN: 978-1-9995949-3-0

First published in 2021

DEDICATION

To all those wonderful people who love planet Earth and the peoples on it.

To my friends who believe in my experiences, no matter how crazy.

To Roy Breeze and Lou Fowles, who helped me get started.

To all those wonderful people who sat for hours with me while I channelled.

Other books by Shirley Battie

Calling Earth	Superpowers fight for Dominion over Earth
Calling Earth 11	Time and Space
Calling Earth 111	Fight for Humanity's Future
Spirit Speaks	Questions and Answers on Life
Beyond the Stairs	Invitation to Walk into Other Dimensions
Channelling	Use Your Psychic Powers
Being Human	with Foreword by Mary Rodwell of ACERN

LITTLE OWL CARDS www.littleowlonline.co.uk

Foreword

Love Being A Human is an updated version of my book *Being Human.*

I have done this to relate it to the world of 2021 and because much has been learnt since the first edition a good ten years ago. Much information given then is even more relevant today and is not to be lost. Some names have been changed, but not all. Those readers who recognise some identities will understand.

Another important reason for adding more to the first *Being Human* book is that there seems to be an urgency about the messages within for those who can listen and understand. It is only on reading it again did I realise how much had been given by my unseen friends. It is no longer simply about me and how I got to where I am. I am only the messenger, and if what happened to me in my journey inspires you, then I and *they* are more than happy. It might encourage you when you are asked by your spirit guidance and your gut feeling, to follow even what appears to be foolish.

In researching my notes of the many journeys I have taken I now realise that there are far too many to include in this book which was intended just to be a re-write. So there may be more down the line. No promises!

As an extra note. Please know that reference throughout to The Great White Brotherhood bears no relation to skin colour or race where White is referring to purity.

It is a sad reflection on today's world that I must state this.

CONTENTS

Introduction

I was enjoying a picnic with friends and family when a thought struck me. What would it be like if I lived in the future, or on other worlds? It was a stupid thought for I knew I was living in the present, in the here and now. All the same, I wondered. What would things be like in a hundred years, two hundred years, three hundred years from now? What I did not know was that my thought brought me a response, from where, I do not know. I was about to step into possible futures and other realms of existence. It all began with a thought, a wondering.

People say you should have an investigative mind. Maybe we all get responses to our questions, to our thoughts. Maybe these responses come much later, long after we have forgotten the original thought. That was how it all began for me. A few years later, I would journey through time and space. How could I have guessed that I would be in other countries far away from my home and delving into other worlds, strange worlds, and other realms? I still did not make the connection with that thought. I have long since left behind that day at the picnic.

I have come to call these journeys to other worlds and other times Mind Walking or Mind Reach. All that is required is that you go into meditation and let the mind take you where your spirit and soul wish you to be. It is important to ask to be shown or taken to what your soul wishes you to experience. You *are* there in those other places and feel as alive and real as you would be at home in your time. I now teach this and call it Mind Reach, Mind Walking, or if you wish Meditation. The experiences students are having are amazing.

But I must go back a bit. It was a bright sunny day in Bournemouth, Dorset, England. It was 1991, and after two long and difficult years, I had at last recovered from losing Ernie, the man I was married to and loved for fourteen years, but who had decided he did not love me enough to stay with me.

"I'm leaving you," Ernie declared over the phone from Germany. My heart stopped. This could not be happening. I had no idea this was coming. I already had travel tickets to join him when he took up his new job there and I had begun to learn German in readiness. Totally unprepared I went into shock and dropped the phone onto its stand. I wanted to get away, anywhere, any place, just away. I wanted to run. Is the need to escape and run away what happens to others in similar circumstances?

They say time is a great healer, and eventually I healed. I picked up the pieces and was determined to get on with life. Dear reader, know that even when you think your world has ended, there are great possibilities ahead for you if you keep your head up high and stride forward. I now know that his leaving was the best thing to happen to me. It was a gift without which I could not have done what was intended all along. Thank you, Ernie. During our time together he had taught me to believe in myself and I had become stronger in the process. His leaving, painful though it was turned out to be a blessing. I changed from being shy and submissive to being an explorer in time. My story is how I moved from spiritual and psychic ignorance to an awareness that there is much more to being alive than I had ever dreamed of. If you want to experience other worlds, you too can do this. You can be whatever you want to be. Let it happen. It is a journey well worth having, and I recommend it to all.

I believe we all have teachers to help us through our lives. Not all are comfortable to have in our lives. We have many teachers, each one giving what we need at the appropriate stage on our journey. The words and experiences given to me are now shared with you in these pages. Much of the direction may be applied to you and acted on. I strongly feel that each direction shown is also meant for anybody and not for me alone. I am a messenger. (*Examples in Beyond the Stairs)* The words spoken by spirit are intended to inspire you to action. You may reject or acknowledge them as truth. This is my reality; one I accept as being compelling, true for me and one I wish to share with you. These have been my journeys and experiences, as genuine as they can be. May you be blessed with similar encounters.

Chapter 1

Into a New Life

Feel the air, smell the scent. Live this existence and what you gain will take you forward into the new life. Be in the moment, forever into infinity. Who are you? You are a breath of wind, an essence that permeates all matter, never to be lost. Therefore you are all and yet nothing at all. Only by being in your consciousness can you know all. It matters not whether you are from the Earth or the Stars, for all is the same. You are a vital element of life. *Dr. Po*

People were still arriving even though the hall was already packed. The murmur of voices and shuffling feet reached me as I stood nervously at the side of the stage, with my fingers crossed. I shut my eyes.

"Please, God, give me the words I need. Please, may I be accurate in my interpretation." The presenter introduced me, and the audience fell silent. I looked over a sea of expectant faces and prayed hard that I would deliver the goods. Again I wondered why I put myself through this. What was it that drove me on? Why on earth didn't I just go to work like everybody else and let the world get on with itself? But I knew I could not and would not.

The presenter stopped talking, and it was my turn. I am not very tall, at five feet, and I was grateful there was no lectern to swamp me. I stepped to the front, Knees shaking I looked out over the faces, and began to speak. My subject was communication with the spirit world and with one's soul. At the end of the short talk, a demonstration of clairvoyance was expected. For most people this was what they had come for, not the talk.

"If you don't do clairvoyance," I was told, "we won't get the people in."

We all like to hear something that is personal to us and for us alone, don't we?

This was 1993 in England, and at that time I had no idea that I was to do much more. But I am getting ahead of myself. The main question people ask me when I give a talk is, "How did you know you had this ability and how did you get started?" To answer this question, I must go back to the beginning where one thing led to another, along a series of threads that I knew I had to follow and am still following today as they are given to me by spirit.

My life began in 1934 in Putney, Southwest London, before the Second World War. I was the second eldest in a family of six children. Growing up I was not much to look at, being what I considered to be plain, straight haired, and with spots. These days when I tell people how shy and reserved I used to be they look at me in disbelief, then they fall about laughing and think I am joking. I was five coming up to six when the war and bombing started. After each frightening air raid, we emerged from our Anderson garden shelter and saw whole streets reduced to rubble where there had been houses before.

Soon it was our turn. Huddled together in the candlelight of the shelter, we listened to the airplanes overhead and waited for the silence which followed. These were the dreaded V-2 bombs. I was seven by then, but I knew that kind of silence meant death for someone. The next moment an immense ear shattering noise and blast collapsed our shelter. After a while the *All Clear* siren sounded. Laughing with relief, we realized we were still alive and unscathed. With hearts pounding and our clothes spattered with dirt, we climbed out from what had been our refuge. I wandered through the ruins of the house to where the front door had been. Mum was too busy with the younger children to notice me, and I felt very alone. I stood in silence, looking in bewilderment at the enormous damage to our house and knew we had no choice but to leave. We lived in an area that was bombed time and time again, so we were evacuated to Treorchy, South Wales, leaving my father behind.

I was a little over ten when the war was all over. We returned to London to a disrupted education with school attendance held at a variety of school venues, depending on how damaged they were and how many classrooms were left intact. So began an extremely unhappy period in my life. After school, the local library became my second home, and I spent hours cosseted by books. I thank all those authors who took me into other worlds and broadened my horizons. The library was preferable to being in the middle of my parents' violent rows. It was an escape hole for me. Today I imagine youngsters in similar situations escaping into their computers or iPads. Mum and Dad soon broke up, and this was partly due to long separation that war often brings. I knew from the local gossip that he had fathered more than one child in the street while we were absent during the war.

It took many years before I could remember my dad without being overwhelmed by fear of him after I witnessed him trying to kill my mother. I have never been able to talk to a soul about events in that period of my life without breaking down in tears. I keep these memories well buried. It is still too painful to be touched, even now as I write these words.

What terrible thing had my father done to me? Nothing. He had not abused or hurt me in any way. I was favorite of all his children he said. He loved me. So why was I terrified of him? Was it witnessing terrible rows and violent scenes between my parents or listening to my mother discussing him endlessly with friends, in terms of fear, hate, and loathing? There was the time I remember the most. "I'll kill you if you leave me!" he shouted at her. I watched him grab her by the hair and pull her to the ground. As she struggled to get up, he hit her hard over the head with a metal bar. Her screams filled the house as he left the room. I learned later that the only thing that saved her was the steel Alice band she always wore. He could have faced a murder charge but for that and I would have been without a mother.

But leave she did, taking all six children with her, the youngest just a small baby. The following years were filled with intense, relentless anxiety that she was in danger. Every sound became a scream in my imagination. I could not focus on school lessons because my ears were constantly on the alert for her screams for help. I became withdrawn, all my concentration reserved for danger signals. I did not smile very often and even now tears well up at the memory as I write.

Many years have passed since that time, and I can now understand the actions of both my parents. I ask all parents who part, for whatever reason, not to belittle and blacken each other in front of, or in hearing of their children. The damage can be great and may last all their lives. With so many families breaking up these days, we may be left with a generation of disturbed children and adults if care is not taken. My own parents never knew what damage they were inflicting.

We moved to another part of Putney, to a war requisitioned house closer to Roehampton in the southwest of London. This was considered to be the posh part. My mother was worn out as she desperately tried to hold the rest of the family together, the youngest being only six months old. She did not look as if she had the strength to go on, and I worried about her constantly. It was 1945, and she did a good job considering there was no state benefit, no payment from my father, and no income support or National Health Service at that time. We wore secondhand clothing donated by better-off families where she did the cleaning. I did not appreciate until much later just how brave she was or how terribly hard it must have been for her. I often heard her crying in her room at night and wished I could do something.

Like all things, the years of hardship passed, and at sixteen, I left school and went to work at Lloyds Bank, known as Cox and Kings in Lower Regent Street, London. I still had no idea of what was to come. Thank goodness for that! If I had known of the difficulties that were ahead of me, I might not have wanted to continue. When people come to me for readings asking what their future holds, I try to keep their focus on the present and what is going on in their lives right now. They often say, 'don't tell me anything bad.' Of course I would not. Most of us will and do manage to work through the challenges that life throws at us as and when they arrive.

I married young at nineteen, full of hope and determination to be a good wife. Seventeen years and three children later, it was clear that it was not going to work, no matter how hard I tried. When people tell me that divorce is too easy, they do not know what they are talking about. Leaving my husband was the hardest decision I ever had to make. Although it was the best thing I have ever done for my children's mentality it led to real struggles to survive alone with the children still in school.

Five years later, I married again. Neither of my marriages was easy, despite a lot of good times. There are good times in any situation. I had three lovely children that I would not have had otherwise. Looking back, I bless both my husbands for the gifts of courage, strength, and I hope, wisdom that I could not have gained without them. I bless them for the emotional experiences, such as extreme despair, unhappiness, and hard work, which most would see as negative gifts. These experiences are the very things that have strengthened me. They help me do my work today with understanding and compassion toward others. I also bless them for the good times, the joys, the love, and in particular, the encouragement from my second husband, who brought me out of my shell. I bless them for forcing me into situations where I had to choose to sink or swim. I chose to swim.

It was during the second marriage that the spirit world began to contact me. The problem was that I did not recognize their attempts. It began in 1977 in northern Italy where my husband Ernie and I were working. To survive financially and to get Ernie out of debt, it was necessary for me to do two full-time jobs. From 8:00 a.m. till 6:00 p.m., I worked as technical editor on helicopter manuals for Augusta. At 6:00 p.m., I would dash from there to work at a variety of venues organised by an English language school until 10:00 p.m., not getting home until 11:00 p.m. most evenings. I managed to do this for eight years.

The spirit world's attempt to contact me started one night when the sky was alive with stars. I finished my day's work and parked the car below our condominium. My bag was heavy with books as I walked to the lift that would carry me to our apartment. As I fumbled for my key, the door opened. Ernie was waiting and had a cup of tea and a light snack prepared for me. He was always considerate and caring. This was our usual routine. We chatted about our respective days and then went to bed.

One night I did not read as usual but decided to go straight to sleep. Ernie was quickly in dreamland, and I was drifting there, when words suddenly spread themselves across my mind. It was just like reading ticker tape. The punctuation and each letter clear in my head. I could see titles to paragraphs. Assuming it was my mind still at work, I tried to switch it off. I tried everything, but the words kept coming. I knew I needed more sleep and got angry at my inability to stop the sentences appearing. "Go away! I want to sleep," I said to my mind.

Whatever it was that intruded did not go away. The string of words continued almost every night for two years. It was like reading a book in my mind, seeing each letter clearly. Not having any knowledge of spiritual matters or spirit connections, I did not put two and two together.

I began to read more and more. I was drawn to books on life after death, books by Dr. Immanuel Velikovsky, and the famous sleeping prophet, Edgar Cayce. One book in particular saved me in a period of extreme distress over my husband's behaviour when drunk and when his change from being kind and loving to one that was anything but loving. This book was *Testimony of Light by Helen Greaves*. It saved my sanity and enabled me to understand and go on.

I was intrigued by the concept of nonphysical worlds and possible existence in other times and dimensions across the universes. The prospect of reincarnation fascinated me. I held discussion groups in my home to talk on these subjects at weekends, feeding my mind with material that would prove to be invaluable later. Curious about the properties of pyramids, I constructed them out of strong card. Not being mathematically endowed, I enlisted help to get the correct measurements and alignment from a group of nuclear physicists that I was teaching. The results of my experiments were impressive. Despite all this, it never crossed my mind to meditate or get more integrally involved.

A visit to a medical consultant during one of our annual journeys home to England for Christmas brought a surprise turn of events. I sat nervously in the waiting room after earlier tests and wondered what the results would be. I passed the time looking at all the certificates on the wall. Eventually, the consultant called me in. He put his hand on my shoulder as I went through the door; just in case I run away, I thought to myself.

"Sit down, please," he said. "No doubt about it, you will need a hysterectomy. When can you come in?" I went blank and could not think for a moment. This was unexpected. I did not hear the rest of the conversation although I know it took place. Because of our financial struggles, we decided it would be best to have the operation over the Christmas period. That way I would not lose my income from the evening teaching job. The day job and medical expenses were covered by company insurance and gave me three months off work. The operation was successful, and a couple of days after I left hospital and flew back to Italy and was back at the evening teaching job on the Monday.

"I'm bored," I told Ernie some weeks later. "I need something to do while I am home during the day." I was accustomed to working flat out. An idea took hold. Why not take a correspondence course in writing, and perhaps I would get some sleep without the nightly interruption of words through my mind? That did the trick. From that moment on, I was left to sleep in peace. The training had begun, but I did not know it was just the beginning.

Chapter 2

One Door Shuts and Another Opens

Be aware of the many events in your life that are leading you towards the final goal that is now in sight. You will find past acquaintances oft forgotten will surface again and make contact. Make the most of these occurrences since they are being impressed to contact you. Do not hesitate to put yourself at their disposal with your gifts. We will arrange the information they seek and you will find there are others as yet unknown to you who will come forward to receive clarity of thought.

From The Little Owl Cards

Both our employment contracts In Italy came to an end, and Ernie took up work in Holland for one year. This led to work in France for two years, and everything looked rosy. But my life with him was coming to an end. It was 1988 and we went home to UK for Christmas, with no hint of a problem between us. He was between contracts and planned to travel to Germany on his way to a new appointment there. I was to join him from England and arrange the removals of our belongings from France to Germany and I began to learn German. I had no inkling of his real plans until that devastating telephone call.

"I'm leaving you," he said. There was no build up or preliminaries. Stunned, I put the phone down and felt sick. Out of consideration for him, (*though he is now on the other side)* I will not go into details of what happened after that.

Divorce followed and I was single again, back home in England and very alone. I did not know anyone, having been out of the country for so many years. There was no other way but to pick myself up and start life over. Luckily, I was able to get a good job even though I was past fifty. I joined an evening counseling course where they meditated at the commencement of each session. I had previously thought that people who meditated were a little weird. The beads and bangles brigade I called them. But at the course they were nice, normal, comfortable individuals. Nothing weird about them, I decided.

It was time to try meditation by myself. I was a little nervous since I had no idea what might happen or if I was doing it right. I chose a night when nothing much was happening, and I relaxed as much as possible. My mind drifted, one thought following another, reminding me of the chain of events that led to this moment. What would my family say if they could see me now? They were scattered around the country. My daughter was then working in Italy, one son in Yorkshire, and the third too far away, and unknown to me was living his own personal hell. They would probably tell me not to mess with things I did not understand. In my mind I heard again my youngest saying with tight lips, "At your age, Mum, you ought to know better." Your age indeed! What did *he* know? Fiftyish is young these days.

My independent mind reminded me, "*You know you don't have to be bullied by a domineering man ever again as his father had done.*" No more being timid, frightened to put a point of view. In my first marriage, I had withdrawn into my shell and cringed every time his voice was raised in anger. According to my husband, it was not only children who were to be seen and not heard, but wives too. I had come a long way since those days and reckoned I had grown enough to do whatever I wanted without anyone else making a fuss. Good grief, I was only meditating. Where was the crime in that? I smiled at my thoughts. Life had been anything but dull, quite exciting really. I would show them. As I sat in my comfortable chair, I realized my mind had wandered off. I was told that happened with beginners at meditation.

A young man's voice crashed into the silence of my mind. "We have been waiting for you." My heart thumped wildly with shock. I was on my own. Why had I attempted to do something I did not understand?

"Who are you? What do you want?" My voice shook. I waited.

I had not really expected anything. I had hoped, yes, hoped that something would happen, but was this right? Heart beating hard, I wished I had left it alone now. Is this what usually happened in meditation? I did not dare move. I heard the little noises of the house. They seemed louder than before. My senses were on acute awareness. The refrigerator hummed gently in the background, the clock ticked, the gas jet in the heating system occasionally puttered. Minutes ticked by. I listened hard, mouth open, half hoping, half fearful. Nothing came. Perhaps it *was* my imagination after all. After what seemed an age I calmed down again and felt foolish.

"Ree-laax!" The voice came again, startled me, and threw me back into the now.

"How can I relax when you make me jump like that?" I protested in my thoughts.

"I am sorry." The voice was softer and gentle now. "We can take you back to live your past again if you wish."

I thought hard and kept my eyes tightly shut. Had he been tapping into my private thoughts? Perhaps this was normal in meditations. I had no previous experience to go on. Who on earth was he? I giggled at a strange thought. Could be he was not of the

Earth! Apprehension slipped away as interest took over.

"Could you really? Look, I am not scared. It is just that you gave me no warning before speaking. Sneaking up and making me jump out of my skin is no way to help me ree-laax," I said, mimicking his accent.

"I will be more careful next time."

"Next time? Who are you anyway?" I asked, curiosity getting the better of caution. My heart settled down to a normal beat. After all, hadn't I said my prayers and asked for protection from negative forces before sitting down to meditate, as instructed in the book I had read? As long as I trusted in divine goodness, I had nothing to fear, it said. Sitting in my own chair at home, I felt safe enough. I knew that I could end this simply by opening my eyes. *If* I wanted to. I did not want to. It was then I realized with a shock that I could mentally see with my eyes shut.

"Who are you?" I repeated.

"All in good time. First, do you want to understand how you came to speak to us? If so, stay quiet and ree-laax. I will take you back six months. I think you will cope with that all right."

The clock on the wall ticked gently on. A long period of silence followed. My mind drifted once more.

Suddenly, I was standing alone by my car, gazing up at the sky thick with stars. I had just left the evening course on counseling. I wrapped a thick scarf more tightly round my neck and shivered in the cold crisp air. The vast canopy of sky looked down on me. How insignificant I was, one solitary human being on one tiny planet in a vast expanse of other worlds, other times. It did not matter to those worlds that I worked myself silly during the day and went on to attend counseling classes in the evenings, or that my own private world had shattered into fragments, each piece sharp and jagged, still able to wound.

I felt desolate and lonely standing by myself in the darkness of the car park. My throat tightened and ached with memories. The tears came, tears I could not stop. I brushed wet cheeks with the back of my gloved hand, grateful there was no one to see. Why did Ernie, my real love, leave me after so many struggles to finally get things right between us? I was sure we had succeeded after fourteen years of trying. I had felt secure and sure of his love.

I could not have been more wrong. I was alone once again, back home in England after so many years away. Friends were as shocked as I was over the breakup of our marriage. I shivered. Perversely I did not want the whole memory to vanish.

"Hello, hello! Are you in there?" The voice came again, an amused voice. I was jolted back to the present time. This was one heck of a comedian. But I grinned in spite of myself. I liked him, liked his sense of humor.

"You know if I told anyone about this they'd lock me away. Is meditation always like this?" I asked.

"Not exactly," he said. "You can use the word meditation if you like, but this is something a little different. We have used a process similar to meditation to make the connection. It took us a long time to get to you."

"I didn't know you existed," I said.

"Hmm! Well! No comment! I forgot that you have to start afresh this lifetime."

What was he talking about now? He did jump about a bit.

"You do not remember the abilities you had in earlier times? No, of course not. Stupid of me," he said lightly.

I was confused. "Who are you anyway? You sound quite human, normal, apart from your funny accent." The presence of him in the room crept like a cold draught around my legs. Perhaps if I opened my eyes? No, better not, it was too risky.

"We will come to my identity later," he said. "First we must deal with your training."

"Training? Training for what?"

"Oh dear! There I go again, saying too much too soon. They should have picked someone else for this job. I told them, but they wouldn't listen." I had the suspicion he was putting on an act to make me feel comfortable.

I felt rather than saw him draw himself up. I now realise that simply knowing what he is doing without actually seeing is quite usual. Assuming a tone of mock importance, he stated, "I have been allocated the responsibility of introducing you to an organization we will call the Communicators for now, sometimes called the Great White Brotherhood or The Ascended Masters. I am one known as Janus, and I represent beginnings and peace."

At last, a name! With a point of reference, I felt more comfortable.

"I feel this is sufficient for you to digest at this time. I will come again, with your permission." His voice grew faint and distant. The intense pressure in my head began to clear. I did not want him to go. It was just beginning to get interesting.

"Don't go. I've a lot of questions. Should I meditate to fetch you?"

He said, faintly now, "We would like you to—er—meditate twice a day if you can. I will go now." With that he left as suddenly as he had arrived. The room felt empty without him. The cold left my legs. I became aware of the ticking clock. A lorry rumbled by outside. A dog barked at the night. That was how it all began.

Chapter 3

Enter the Glowing One

I was hungry for more. More confident and comfortable with the procedure, I sat again next day. I said a prayer to protect me from any negative influences or thoughts. The now-familiar charge of energy surged in, filling my head as I relaxed. I mentally asked to be taken where they needed me to be.

Soon my bare feet felt crisp yellowing grass beneath my toes, the sort of grass one gets after a long hot, dry spell. A scorching sun beat on my head and burned the back of my neck. I saw a wooden hut in front of me. I wriggled my toes and enjoyed the scrunch of dried grass before climbing up two rough-hewn steps to the hut. It was time to explore. I slowly pushed the wooden door open and cautiously went in. Peering through the musty gloom, I saw a figure sitting at a table. I gasped with delight for he glowed with a luminosity that reminded me of an old painting in which the main figure stands in a pool of light. The beautiful young man brushed shoulder-length hair back from his face with long delicate fingers. He wore a gold band around his head with a cobalt blue stone set in a triangle hanging just above his eyes. "*Now there's a man,*" I breathed. With the gentlest of smiles, he looked at me without surprise and beckoned me to sit down. Struck dumb by his beauty, I sat in a daze, facing him across the rough table.

He began to speak softly, kindly, as if to a child, "At last we meet, my dear one. One role you have been given is to be a source of reassurance to those who are distressed. You are to calm frightened beings, those who will not know what is happening and who will not know what they must do. You will be there to guide, to direct, and to reassure.

"There are many who do not believe there is anything beyond their current lives. Those souls who do not believe will have no anchor to cling to when their materialistic world is thrown into a heap. Show them that there is a point within them that will give them strength. They will be like lost children looking for a light to guide them. You are to prepare now for this role. You will prepare others so that there is a continuation of support for them in years ahead. That is your course, if you choose to take it. You will be helped."

I stared at him dumbfounded, heart pounding. What could I say? I knew I would follow this glorious young man wherever he led me. I would accept this role. I would do anything he asked of me. What was it he said? "*When their materialistic world is thrown into a heap*"? He stood up and began to fade into the dark of the hut. Were his words predictions of hard times ahead?

I felt again soft cushions at my back, supporting me. Realizing my mouth was open, I shut it quickly and swallowed hard. I had not gone anywhere after all. I was back home with the clock ticking monotonously on the far wall. Slowly I opened my eyes and saw the familiar photographs of my family on the mantelpiece. My grown children and grandchildren smiled back at me. Would they care? What would they say if they knew? Would I ever see the beautiful young man again? I wanted to so very much.

Chapter 4

Healing Hands

Walk softly so you do not bruise the tender feelings of your fellow souls. Step lightly through the damaged bodies and tormented minds, casting as you go a soft gentle healing glow. As you pass along, may the breath of your passing be as a balm, a healing, a comfort. *Little Owl Cards*

It seemed I had a role in life. Whoopee! A distant part of me knew it all along. But don't we all have a role? Who was the glorious young man who vanished into thin air? If I had taken drugs, maybe I could understand it, but I had never taken that risk.

Life had to go on, and I had to work. It was 1989. I had been lucky to get a job at my age. The office where I worked became even more demanding. It kept my mind from dwelling too much on the other world that I had entered so easily. It was difficult to find the time to meditate twice a day since I was often working ten to eleven hours each day. But there was always the weekend, and fortunately, I have always been able to rise early.

I woke to a bright, sunny Sunday morning. I sighed as I looked at the kitchen sink piled with dirty dishes left over from the evening before. The sound of lawn mowers in neighboring gardens filled the air. It felt good to be away from the office and its perpetual problems. I looked at the congealed food on the plates with disgust and wished I had not left them till now. Steaming hot water splashed over the dishes, and I absentmindedly began to clean up.

Suddenly the voice of Janus arrived, catching me off guard. "Hi!" he said.

A plate slipped from my wet hands. "Oh, it's you." I felt foolish standing there, dishcloth in hand, not knowing what to say to a disembodied voice. Thank God I was alone.

"I will be leaving you soon," he said, having just arrived.

"Oh," I said again, not very intelligently. I felt heaviness in my heart. It was to be ended after all.

"Someone else is coming to take over. He is to help you with the healing."

That got my attention. "Healing? Healing what, and who?" How he loved dropping bombshells!

"You will see," he said mysteriously. "My part in connecting you is exceedingly small. From now on, there will be some changes. I have come just to prepare you. I told you that before, didn't I?"

"Changes, what changes?"

"Umm! Like I said, healing. Oh yes, and you will see who you are communicating with."

As calmly as I could, I said, "Can you please be more specific?" Didn't he know I had already *seen* the glowing one?

"You will see. The next communicator will explain. He has more experience than I, and more authority." With that, he left abruptly.

I did not want to wait. That evening, I eagerly sat down to meditate and tried not to think of Janus. After a while, I became aware of a presence.

"Ahem!" it said, as if clearing the throat. "Ahem! Good evening."

I saw him in my mind. He was a short, rounded Mongolian with flattened round face and high cheekbones. He wore a distinctly jovial appearance, and around his almond eyes were deep laughter lines. A flat hat sat jauntily on straggly hair. A thin drooping moustache did nothing to cover his smile. I suppressed a giggle and studied him in silence. I waited for him to speak.

"I have been sent." He gave a low theatrical bow. "Allow me to introduce myself. I am known as Wang Lu, the talkative one. A good one to have for communicating, eh? Eh? Eh?"

Another comedian, I decided. Had they been handpicked to put me at ease or what? Surely he couldn't be the one to do with healing?

"But of course, we wish you to be at ease," he said, waving his arms about wildly. Oops! He had read my thoughts.

"Yes, I am to arrange matters so that you become versed in ways of healing, both mind and body. We must start the training at a basic level, though I have been given to understand that you are already aware of what is required. That *is* right, isn't it?"

"Uh, I am not sure what you mean by aware," I stammered,

not sure how to deal with him.

He squinted at me. "I am told you have had experience of many things in previous times."

"If you say so." It was easier to agree. My head was spinning.

"As I said, I shall arrange situations to bring back memories of healing capacities that you had once before." He spread his arms wide. "Look!"

Immediately I entered a long hospital corridor with shiny, polished floors reflecting many pastel colours. I walked along, looking into each room. People lay on beds, each one bathed in a colour. A man came out of one of the rooms. It was Wang Lu himself, chirpy, cheerful, and decidedly roguish. With a shock, I realized I was an older, rather plump woman, grey haired and entirely different from me as I am now. My hands were old and careworn. Wang Lu threw chubby arms round me and hugged me warmly. Together we walked until the scene faded.

Then we were back. Wang Lu stood facing me, a happy grin on his face, his legs planted wide, looking just like a tubby pirate. "You see! We can take you forward and backward in time, as we said. For the present, we will place a screen before you, which you will enter. We will do this in easy stages until you are able to do without." He grinned, showing a full set of astonishing white teeth, gesturing as he spoke. Trying to follow his wild movements, I forgot to listen to the words. He made me giddy.

"I have had connections with you in past times, as you have seen. That being so, I have detailed knowledge of your capabilities. We place great emphasis on learning as much as possible in each lifetime, for what is learnt remains for all time." He grinned ear to ear, turned away, and was gone.

The place felt empty without his tremendously energetic presence. The room was thick with silence. I stretched and yawned, tired now. There was a lot to think about.

Confirmation of Wang Lu's words came quickly. It was during the course on counseling that I met Roy, a short rotund figure with a full head of very white hair. He had a presence that nobody could ignore. Not one to keep quiet, he made himself known to me at the first class. We seemed to have the same sense of humor and both giggled at the same inappropriate time. I did not know then that he had been a medium for over twenty years. We knew what the other was thinking at any time. It was Roy who explained what had been happening to me and it was no surprise to him that these contacts were made.

"I know about these things," he explained a little pompously. "What you are doing is entering another dimension through an altered state."

I was not sure what he meant, but it was a great relief to know that I wasn't mad, that others like me had similar experiences. He arranged for me to have a reading, which I discovered is a consultation with a medium. This was a first for me. I had no idea what to expect.

He booked an appointment with Josefina. I liked her immediately. She was tiny, with long dark hair, and had a wonderful smile. I was glad it was being recorded for the words came quickly.

"You should be doing my work by now, my love," she said. "Do you not know what degree you came with? You were a medium before. You are a healer, a clairvoyant and important channel to the world, and a medium. You will work in public and do automatic writing." She rattled on, hardly pausing for breath until at last she ran out of steam and switched off. "There, my love. Has that helped you? "You've done it all before. You just need polishing up, that's all."

That is all? I thought. How would I go about it? I left the cottage, my head spinning.

The next move came from spirit. "Phone Lou Fowles," an internal voice prompted. Why on earth should I do that? I had only met him once at a lecture when we'd exchanged business cards, simply because we had the same birthday but ten years apart. I ignored the insistent voice.

The unseen "*they*" were not going to give up so easily. Each day as I drove to work, the voice persisted. "Phone Lou Fowles." After two weeks of this, I gave in. I picked up the phone and called the number on the card.

"Mr. Fowles, I need to see you. When can I come over?" An appointment was made for later that week. What was I to say to him? A voice told me to come? He would certainly think I was crazy.

Lou opened the door as I walked up the path. "I don't really know why I am here," I said nervously.

"I do," he said. "You are to learn the methods of healing. Come inside and we'll talk."

I followed him into a little room, clearly set up as a healing center with a therapy couch in the middle of the room. Lou was a large warm and friendly man who made me feel comfortable.

He looked at me and smiled. "I knew you would come eventually," he said. "I was told by my unseen friends that you would. Please sit down."

So he too had communication from the spirit world. Relieved, I settled back into the chair.

"Let me explain. I run the healing center in this area. I am qualified by the NFSH (National Federation of Spiritual Healers) to give you instruction. If you want it," he added.

If *they* had gone to all this trouble, I decided, then I would go ahead. "Agreed," I said.

Arrangements were made for training once a week after

work. A lot was learned over the next few months. Many lessons were given from spirit. A man called George came regularly for healing. I treated him as kindly and attentively as possible, but in my heart I could not warm to him. Despite this, George told me that the healing was having a beneficial effect. I reflected on his problems during a meditation, hoping to find a solution for him.

A voice broke into my reverie. "The lovable ones are easy to love, but it is the unlovable ones who need your love the most. If you cannot love your patients, then you cannot be a healer."

It was the voice of the glowing one Andreas, the kind one. I had a lot to learn. I had to feel compassion for suffering, without judging. Healing cannot, must not be a routine procedure, I realized. However, George was no longer needed healing in the physical sense. He needed counseling. I told him this was so. He never came again.

A month later, after a hard day at work, I turned the key in the front door as the telephone was ringing. It was a friend. Her distress was obvious.

"Shirley, please help me! John has been rushed into hospital with a heart attack. Can you do something? Please! He might die. He is in intensive care. It is serious. Please ask for healing for him. Do what you can."

"Now calm down, I'll ask for healing tonight at 10:00 p.m. That's a promise." I replaced the receiver. It was 8:30 p.m. I prayed he would not die. John was a good man; he would be missed if he left so soon. Lou had explained all about this form of healing called absent or distant healing when a sick person and the healer cannot be together. Dear God, please help him, I begged.

That night, as promised, I took myself into a relaxed state and prayed for the healing energies to be directed to John. I could mentally see his body laid out on a bed with all the tubes and wires of the intensive care unit attached to him. To my amazement, a shower of what appeared to be silver dust particles began falling over him. I knew without being told that it was my job to keep this vision going for as long as possible without losing it. After what seemed a long time, the shower of silver faded. It was finished. I knew that all would be well, but I decided to pray and ask for help each evening.

John, home only a few days later, was the next one to phone me. He was excited. "I have to tell you. When I was in hospital, I saw a stream of silver dust all over me. Just like a shaft of sunlight with dust particles in it, but there were no windows and no sun, no place it could have come from. It was magical." After a chat, I put the phone down, thrilled. What wonderful proof that absent healing works!

Word spread. The healing list grew longer and longer. I quickly discovered that not all were to be healed. I was sometimes told by an inner voice, "Do not disturb." Either that person was not to be healed or, on a deeper level, did not really want to be. There were those who held on tightly to their infirmity or pain, as a necessary part of their lives. I later realized that some souls have chosen to have a particular illness, to either experience and overcome it, or to help in the growth of their loved ones.

The weeks flew by, and I settled into a routine.

"Let's go window-shopping, Mum," suggested my daughter, now living back in UK. We got in the car and set off. We stood admiring shoes in a shop window, when a woman from the other side of the street made a beeline for us across a road heavy with traffic. We both saw her coming.

"Do you know her, Mum?" my daughter asked as the woman approached.

"Never seen her before in my life," I whispered.

The woman reached us and touched me on the arm. "I have a terrible headache," she said. She was breathing quickly and was screwing her face up in pain. Surprised, I mumbled something suitable and put my hand on the woman's forehead.

I had to say something. "You don't seem to have a temperature," I said. "Perhaps it's the heat." Silently, I was asking for healing from Source. A moment passed. The woman beamed, then departed, saying she felt better. Her headache had gone. We never saw her again.

My daughter looked at me curiously. "I wonder why she came to you. Does this sort of thing happen often?"

"I can't imagine," I lied. "Perhaps it's because they like my face," I said laughing. If this sort of thing took place with the family around, it would soon come out what I was involved in. I was not ready for that yet. I knew my youngest son would certainly not approve.

The beautiful glowing one from the hut surprised me by paying another visit soon after. This time I recovered myself sufficiently to ask, "Who are you?"

"I am Andreas," he said quietly. He looked at me steadily with eyes of an incredible blue. There was strength and gentleness about him. His kindness was unmistakable. I tried hard not to break down and cry. How many of us well up when someone shows such loving kindness to us? It is sad that we are not used to such love.

"Listen to me," he said. "Through you, we are to speak to many. You too are to be kind to people. Imagine *you* are the person you are seeing and treat accordingly. You are to have an understanding of others and put yourself in their place."

He waited while I took this in. He put his hand on my shoulder. "A hand on the shoulder or an arm can be sufficient to comfort somebody. Touch when you can, or when you feel it is needed. Healing is not only for the physical body. There are many opportunities for this form of comforting. There will be opportunities if your eyes are open. Do not be so involved with your own thoughts and activities that you do not see the needs of others. Allow people to unburden themselves, in the knowledge that they will not be commanded or required to act in a certain way. Listen with love." He removed his hand from my shoulder and took my hand in his.

"Why are you giving me this direction?" I asked looking down at my feet.

"You will be approached more and more," he answered gently. "Do not be afraid to take the challenges offered. We will assist you. Do not continue to doubt yourself." He raised my chin with his finger. An exquisite shiver of pleasure passed through me.

"First, you must develop. Go out and talk to as many people as you are able. Talk not about yourself. Be interested in the daily happenings of others. This will bring great reward to them and indirectly to you. Do not be afraid to approach people."

"Why me? I mean, why are you all putting so much effort into teaching me?"

"We need one who is not limited by family restrictions. You have pledged yourself to work for humanity. We are taking you up on that pledge."

My heart beat faster. "Are you one of the Great White Brotherhood" I asked.

"I will leave that for you to decide." His gentle voice gave nothing away. I was no wiser than before. "I will tell you that the organization is vast," he added mysteriously. He turned away, fading like a wispy cloud, and was gone. I sighed. He was right; I did not have family restrictions. My mother had died after my return to England. I had brought my children up to be independent, and I no longer had a man in my life. I *was* alone.

Since that time giving healing has taken yet another turn. In addition to, or instead of the usual healing methods, my connection with our Cosmic Cousins has strengthened and they have taught me how to speak their language. Some call this Light Language but I think of it as Cosmic Language. They explained that the sound of it has a vibration which when appropriate heals those who hear it and feel the vibration. I am now able to teach this and realise it does so much more than that. I write about this in my books *Calling Earth. 1, 11 111*

Chapter 5

Training Begins

See the centre of light deep within your being,
for that is your soul.
Observe this light as if watching from a point
outside of yourself.
You will be amazed at how beautifully it shines.
Take time to wonder at it and ask where it may
have been before this life and where it may yet go.
Remind yourself of the source of its birth where all
life begins, and you will rest serene.
The Little Owl Cards, The White Brotherhood

It had been an ordinary day like any other. I could not know this was the evening I would never forget. It was still light outside. It was high summer. A blackbird's song rang echoing through the treetops, sending a thrill through me as it always did. I sat down to meditate a little earlier than usual.

A delightful warmth began to grow from the center of my body. It grew until it completely engulfed me and went beyond, out into the room. It was love, utter and complete love. I was in and surrounded by love with an ecstasy that was way beyond mere physical sensation, and yet it was orgasmic and physical too. This was an all-encompassing love coming from somewhere with a much greater intensity than any mortal could give. I felt I was loved by God. Enfolded in the most exquisite rapture, I did not want it to end, *ever*. I wanted more, more, more.

It ended at last. I pulled myself together with a huge effort. I tried to stand, but my legs buckled under me. I was unable to walk. Tears of joy streamed down my cheeks. It was ten minutes before I gained enough strength to move. I struggled to my feet and had to lean against the wall of the room for support. Trembling all over, I doubted if I would ever be the same person again. Was that what was meant by a Divine experience, a vision of God? I felt I had met God. I wanted to stay with him. I would do anything to have that experience again. What was it? I had to know.

Others saw the effect of it on me. The following evening I walked into the adult education class on philosophy that I was attending, to be greeted by the tutor, "Shirley, whatever have you done to yourself?" I looked down at my clothes to see if I had spilled anything on them. "You are positively glowing," she said.

It was the same in the office. "Who is the new boyfriend then?" My boss winked knowingly.

"I haven't got a boyfriend," I answered laughing.

"Nobody looks like that unless there's a new boyfriend on the scene. You can't fool an old dog like me."

All week it was the same. People and friends wanted to know what wonderful thing had happened to set me aglow. How could I tell them? They would think I had gone off my rocker. Everywhere I went, people smiled broadly at me. It was a wonderful time. I was enjoying life and bursting with happiness. This was living.

At the office, the girls quizzed me. They imagined I had a mysterious past and wanted to know what I did in the evenings. I never spoke about my private life to them and they were determined to find out.

"What did you get up to last night?" Cynthia, a coworker asked, a little too casually, as I tapped energetically on my keyboard. Pretending disinterest, I kept my eyes fixed on the monitor screen.

"Go on. Do tell," chipped in Julie, whose ears were always open. "Who've you been seeing?" They all seemed to think that as I was alone I was not complete until I had "someone special" in my life.

I would give them something to think about, I decided. "I've made an appointment to have a reading," I said, deliberately being mysterious.

"What's that when it's at home?" asked Julie.

"You know, when you are told things about yourself and your future," I said.

A snort and a giggle came from Marian. "Perhaps you'll be told who you're going to meet. Someone tall, dark, handsome, and rich."

"Don't be daft," I muttered, more to myself than to the others.

Cynthia took her eyes away from the screen in front of her. "I don't believe in all that stuff. Getting involved with the devil, that's what that is." Sharp disapproval edged her voice. Her lips pressed tight together in a prim line.

"I'm not worried. I have not come to any harm so far, and I do not suppose listening to another human being is going to hurt me. All the people I've met so far who involve themselves in *that sort of work* have been more friendly and warm than many others I know." I threw her a meaningful look.

I was more determined than ever to go now, if only to prove them wrong. Even so, I was not prepared for what was to come. The time soon arrived for my meeting with Eve Payne, a medium. I arrived at the address given and stood on the mat outside the door.

The door opened to reveal a cheerful, friendly woman. I discovered later that she worked at the SAGB (Spiritualist Association of Great Britain) in London.

"Come in, come in, dear," she beamed. Soon with a cup of tea beside me, I listened intently as she began.

"I have a guide here who says he's been with you for a very long time. His name is Abdul el- Faraz." She told me that he had to make good the way he had treated me in a past life. Until he had done that, he could not move on himself. Her eyes glazed over while she continued to elaborate, with dates and events to do with my personal life. I was amazed she could know so much. One hour later, I stood up, thanked her, and in rather a daze, walked out of the building into a biting cold wind to ponder over all that had been said. What was extraordinary was to be told yet again what I was expected to do in this lifetime. I was to give readings and communicate with an unseen spirit world. It made me think. Did this mean that guides sent to help us could not move on themselves until they had fulfilled their task? Or were some guides with us simply because of past lives together and were in our same soul group, helping each other? Then there were the teachers, not classed as guides. And where did the angels fit in? I had so much to learn before the Cosmic Cousins made themselves known to me. I often call them *Extra-Celestials.*

It was all very impressive. There was more to life than I had ever imagined. I had always believed that life did not end with death and that the spirit is able to communicate from the other side, but I never would have guessed in my wildest imaginings that I had abilities to make these connections myself. Abdul had said meditation was to be my communication link. How right he was, but where was all this leading? Was I really safe in following unseen voices? Was I going mad?

I was in two worlds. One was filled with office work, with

panic situations as a norm. Bills had to be paid and housework done. These were the realities of current life and kept my feet on the ground. My other world was secret, only shared with Roy, who understood and who was always keen to hear of my next episode. I began to see with new eyes, as if I had never really seen anything before. Each contact with spirit became an adventure. I asked masses of questions and received answers to them all. Unfortunately, I forgot what I had asked and details of the answers I received. I decided it was a pity if this happened each time and something had to be done about it. I considered it futile if I lost the information. I wasted no time in asking.

Andreas the glowing one came again. "Good morning," he began gently.

I melted. Secretly I called him my angel, though I would have been embarrassed to tell this to anyone, even to Roy.

"Hello," I answered, smiling at my thoughts.

He smiled back. I realized too late that he knew what I was thinking. Flustered, I got down to the matter in hand and explained how it was. "What can I do about it?" I asked.

His voice was quiet and calm. "Record it. Put it on tape."

Just that! Of course! What an idiot I was. I could have thought of that myself.

He went on, "Words are representations of feelings and thoughts. They are useful in that they can be held up and examined more clearly. Thoughts alone can escape and are sometimes difficult to stay in the mind." He understood my frustration exactly.

I tried to do what Andreas had suggested but was not satisfied with the results. It was time to call on them for more help. Getting into my meditation once more, I was glad to see Andreas and Wang Lu arriving together.

I put a question to them, or more correctly, a grumble. "I did what you told me and recorded my sessions," I said. "I go straight to the tape recorder, but it's like telling someone a story, or telling a friend about a film I've seen. It is incomplete and I forget large chunks of the conversation. I cannot put over the emotions or feelings I get during the time I'm with you. What I am saying is, I am not satisfied."

They looked at each other and said nothing. Wang Lu grinned broadly. Andreas tried to look sympathetic but only succeeded in smiling. His blue eyes sparkled. I felt he wanted to laugh. I knew they had both anticipated this and were not surprised by my outburst.

"No problem," they said in unison.

"You first," Andreas said politely.

"Thank you." Wang Lu bowed, theatrically sweeping his arm wide. "Why do you not record it as it happens, as we speak?"

I shook my head. "That's not so easy. I am aware that I hear you in my head not with my ears, and I speak to you in my thoughts. How can I record that?" I felt I had scored a point.

"Aha!" they said in unison again.

It was Andreas who spoke next. "We would like you to voice what *we* say *as* we say it and speak aloud what *you* say to us. We will help you."

I blinked. I was prepared to try but knew it would not be easy.

"We would also like you to describe aloud what you see," he continued, watching me carefully. "When you begin to describe, your voice box is activated, and then we can move in and use it. See?"

I did not see. "I'll give it a go," I promised.

At first it was still like describing after the event, but it was better than nothing. Over a short period of time, with practice, I became more adept. I found I could voice what they were saying simultaneously with the thought and did not have to wait, listen, and then speak. I learned to switch over to their minds and use direct speech. I was aware they were using my mind to articulate their own thoughts, and I did not know in advance what they intended to say until the words were out. It was strange but not unpleasant. I found that I could still interact with them and ask questions as I had done before. I forgot that I had a body and that the words produced were coming from my voice box. At last I was getting somewhere. I enjoyed the sessions, but there was still one problem that would not go away.

"It's no good," I complained to Andreas. "You must think I do nothing but complain," I said miserably. "But my work at the office is taking up all my thoughts and energy. Now with the increase in the amount of healing work and longer and longer meetings with you, I have no time left to do other things."

"What other things?" He wrinkled his nose and gazed at me in such a direct way that I melted and went weak at the knees.

"You understand. Things like seeing the news on television, writing letters. All the things one must do to function on this Earth. I have not read a book for simply ages, and I have so many I want to get into. I do not want you to think I am fed up or want to stop our sessions, but it's a big problem. I am torn between duty to the office and everyday life and the amount of time we spend together. Can you organize it so that I have more time? After all, the day only has twenty-four hours in it. Can it be fixed that I manage on fewer hours of sleep and not suffer?" I did not want to suffer. I knew by now he could arrange many things; maybe he could do this too.

"We will see." He was noncommittal.

From then on I woke up each night at 3:00 a.m., fresh as a daisy. At first, I tried to go back to sleep, until it dawned on me that this was the answer to my request for more time. I was able to stay connected with them for an hour at least and then go back to sleep. I suffered no ill effects.

It was a good time to ask yet again if Andreas was one of the White Brotherhood. "Are you one of the White Brotherhood?" I asked bluntly.

"It depends on what you mean by 'brotherhood.' If you mean, do I communicate? Well, yes, I do. If you mean, am I part of that organization? Yes to that too."

I knew he was teasing. He was quite aware of what I was really asking. He had not answered the question to my satisfaction.

In a more serious tone, he went on, "The Communicators are a vast organization more commonly known as the Great White Brotherhood, which has the interest and care of your universe and the peoples in it. Some on your planet call them the Ascended Masters. They have authority to involve humans and nonhumans who have sufficient dedication to apply themselves for the benefit of others."

I was awestruck; my mouth dropped open. "Wow!"

Ignoring the interruption, he continued, "The organization sometimes known as The Galactic Confederation is one of many, controlled by and working for a higher authority. They have influence over and responsibility for the universe in which your solar system exists. We understand this information will bring many more questions to your mind. You will require further clarification of course. First, may we ask you to perfect the art of recording the information given? We have already exceeded our brief in supplying you with this knowledge so soon."

I realized that Andreas was speaking in the plural. Was he a spokesman for many? He spoke with great command. Suitably impressed, I certainly had plenty to think about. Andreas obviously thought so too and quietly left my mind.

Yet more time was needed. Once more, I tentatively again put the problem to my spirit friends. "There's still not enough time to do all the things I want to do," I said.

"What things now?" They looked puzzled.

"You know, all the things you want me to study. The candle burns bright and long, but I don't want to splutter out completely." I thought I had put that rather cleverly and was pleased with myself at my turn of phrase.

"What we have suggested should be easy," they said together. "You have done them all before. It is only revision."

"That's all right for you to say," I retorted. "But I don't remember what happened or who I was before this life. For me it's a new learning." Andreas looked up at the ceiling as if trying to see something above him. He stayed quiet for so long I thought he had forgotten me completely. Then he lowered his head to look at me intently.

"It shall be arranged," he said seriously, "but you might not like the arrangement."

They did not waste any time. Through the post, a week later, arrived a long-awaited appointment with a consultant at the hospital. To my surprise, I was booked in the following week for a major operation to repair damage that had been done because of excessive hard physical work in my first marriage. This gave me three months off work. It gave me the time I had asked for. It had been arranged!

I remembered that when they want me to do something, three months off and away from my normal activities is their preferred method, as it was with the nightly writing in Italy.

Again and again, I would be reminded that what we ask for we get. Mary, a friend of Cynthia's, was constantly asking for a break, since she was overworked. It was her constant cry, "Give me a break." Shortly after that, she broke her arm. She had her break all right. Then there was the lady called Jane. Jane was the mother of a large family with constant demands on her time. She was frequently heard to say, "Oh, how I'd love to be waited on hand and foot, and to have everyone waiting on me for a change." She was soon to suffer an illness, which left her paralyzed. She had to be waited on hand and foot for she could do nothing for herself. I knew I had to be very careful what I ask for and how I ask it. The subconscious simply receives messages we frequently send it and complies in whatever way it can. I was reminded of something sent to me which fitted everything.

I asked for courage and he gave me danger to overcome.
I asked for strength and he gave me difficulties to make me strong.
I asked for Wisdom and God gave me problems to solve.
I asked for health that I might do greater things.
I was given infirmity that I might do better things.
I asked for riches that I might be happy.
I was given poverty that I might be wise.
I asked for power that I might have the praise of men.
I was given weakness that I might feel the need of God.
I asked for all things that I might enjoy life.
I was given life that I might enjoy all things.

About this time during a meditation I was approached by a glorious angel. It was the most amazing experience and left me in awe.

"I will give you a wish" he said. "What would you wish for?"

I thought quickly. I had the healing gift, so I did not ask for that. I had love for all things, so I did not need to ask for love. If I had wisdom then whatever happened in my life I could deal with it wisely.

"I would like wisdom please," I said. He nodded and vanished. Only time will tell if I have any.

Chapter 6

Past and Future Lives

Oh, how the souls cry in their sleep
for peace, love and happiness.
Dear God, grant them what they seek.
Your name forever they will bless.
How can this be, our God replies,
for man himself creates his world.
Do they not know that all their sighs
result from actions now unfurled?
Dear children, listen to me.
If you would have a perfect life,
cease your endless strife and enmity.
from spirit

I am sometimes asked, if I am a healer, why was there a need for my operations? All I can say is, I had ignored the body's warning signs until only an operation could rectify matters. It also gave me what I had asked for, time.

Back home I was stiff and sore after the operation, every movement was an effort. Despite this, I prepared to meet my invisible friends now that I was out of hospital. Roy sat opposite me, ready to operate the tape recorder. Not knowing whether anything would be given under these conditions, I settled down and relaxed.

The energy surged in, and soon I was able as usual to describe the scene I found myself in. I was there, and it felt as real to me as when I am in the office working. I felt gritty sand beneath my feet, with hot dry air blasting my face, tightening the skin. My eyes screwed up against stinging windblown sand.

Me speaking: "I see three Tuaregs on camels riding towards me as the wind dies down. They are very tall, grand, and imposing. I feel small and defenseless. Their faces are wrapped and hidden by cloth. I can only see the eyes. They look at me and dismount. The middle one comes close and puts his hands under my elbows in a greeting. It is a formal embrace. His dark eyes look through me and know me. Such penetrating eyes! The other two are guardians, Guardians of the Way."

The tall one begins to speak in a deep gruff voice, "We have come to escort you, to ensure you reach your goal. You are to be escorted safely so that what you carry reaches the intended destination. It is to be displayed in the correct place at the appointed time. It is not to be lost in the sands of time or buried beneath the shifting sands. It must be kept fresh and vibrant."

I wonder what he is talking about. It is all very obscure. Perhaps it is all about the information they give me. This is strange. There they are, looking resplendent on tall camels, yet I am given a little donkey to ride. They lead me on the donkey. I look a bit incongruous in company with these great people. I want to cry. I am overwhelmed by emotion. I do not know what I am carrying, except that it is precious. We move very slowly and majestically forward. I am overcome with the experience, deeply moved.

With tears streaming down my face, I continue speaking: "I see a little figure in the distance behind me. The little figure on the camel looks so small in comparison to these grand three. He is not coming with us. He is staying where he is. I know for certain it is Abdul el Faraz. He has completed his task and has paid his debt. I break down and weep."

The tallest Tuareg turns around saying, "Wipe your tears. It is a joyous journey you are on." The scene ends. I am returned to the stillness of my room.

Roy was quiet, stunned, and temporarily lost for words. "I wonder what you were carrying in that scenario. No doubt we will find out in due course. You know, Tuaregs are a nomadic people of the west central Sahara. In most Tuareg groups, there are marabouts, a religious class with hereditary holy men who play an important role as arbitrators and conciliators."

I wondered if I was living in cloud-cuckoo-land. Who would ever believe me if I let it be known what I was seeing and hearing? Wasn't it all rather too fantastic? If someone else told me the same story, I would not believe them. I would consider them to be delusional. Was I delusional? Was it just my imagination? Yet it felt real enough. The memory of hot dry sand and the parched taut skin on my face was still with me. I *had been* there. I shook my head, desperate to understand.

I decided to go to yet another medium for a reading, someone who did not know me at all. If I were given the same information, maybe I could believe it.

He turned out to be an elderly gentleman, rather dapper in dress. He spoke quickly and precisely. "First, let me explain about the imagination that you are doubting. The images which you call imagination come from your soul, your subconscious which never lies. It can be used and trusted, even though it may need to be understood or interpreted, it is not often literal. When however you *create* a picture or scene in order to have something, that is making it up and is a deliberate attempt by your logical mind to understand. Imagination is valuable and should not be doubted."

Wow! He really has tapped into my mind with my doubts, I thought.

He smiled and continued. "You are a teacher, a healer, a medium. It is time you used these gifts." He went on to describe both Andreas and Wang Lu. "These two will help you, but there are to be many more, as you progress."

Confidence restored, I settled down to meditate, alone once more. I was to be even more alone in other ways, and this puzzled me for some time.

"Your connection and learning with Roy is to end, and you will go different ways," he said as he escorted me to the door.

Andreas appeared gently before me, softly glowing. "Now, what is all this questioning and doubting?" He knew. Of course, he knew. He knew everything about me.

"I don't mean to doubt," I stammered, "but this is all so unusual. I do not see how I can possibly come up to your expectations. I feel so—so ordinary, so incompetent. I'm not capable at all."

"It has been very quick, I know," he said. "Trust me. We know what we are doing. I would like to take you to experience certain things that will help, if you will agree." It was a statement, not a question.

"There are many like you being prepared."

In my mind, I wondered if he was real or imagination as he moved slowly about the room, touching my books, stroking ornaments, leaving a trail of glowing mist as he went.

"Remember how we took you back to a past time? We will also take you to other times, both forward and back. We will be with you at all moments during these journeys. You will be safe. You will be like a news correspondent, observing and recording so that what you see, hear, and feel may be conveyed to the public. Do we have your permission?"

I nodded dumbly.

"Good. You will visit yourself in other times. Does that worry you at all?"

"No," I said. "It will be very interesting." What an inadequate reply to such a question. I was calm, all things considered, as if this were a perfectly natural and normal thing to be doing.

Andreas looked at me steadily. His blue eyes searched my face for signs of nerves. "Ready?" I nodded.

"Relax, and you will see a large full-length mirror in front of you. Step into this as soon as you see a picture. No matter what you see, go towards it, step into it. It is easy. You will see. Tell me what happens, *as* it happens. You are an on-the-spot reporter. Remember the training."

I relaxed, and after a while, I said, "I see the mirror. It is shimmering, as if a shiver has passed over it. The desert is laid out before me. There is an enormous tent a little way off with tall, fierce-looking guards posted outside. I step through the mirror. Aah! The heat is like a solid wall." I put my hand up to my face to shield my eyes from the glare. As I did this, I saw black hairs on my hand, a man's hand. "What's happening?" I stared in trembling disbelief. I was a young man, strong and virile. I looked down at my clothes, desert robes.

"It is all right. It *is* you," Andreas whispered in my ear. "Go forward."

With that, I lost my present reality as Shirley. I as the young man strode forward, very proud and confident and entered the tent.

"Tell me," commanded Andreas as softly as a breath of wind.

"Many men of all tribes are seated on the ground. They are waiting. Each has a different headdress, each one a leader, strong men. They gesture for me to sit. I am to speak to them."

I, as the youth, begin, "I am here to tell you to stop behaving like irritable monkeys, one tribe against the other. Join and live in peace together. This is something you have seldom done. It is time to stop fighting, brother against brother. There is enough space for all. Stop the bloodshed and the hate. You are gathered here together as many tribes as possible from across the nations to pledge peace and unity. You must live in harmony if you are to survive, if you are to work for the benefit of all mankind, not only for the Arab nations. Put an end to selfishness and greed."

A mixture of grunts and murmurs rippled through the tent.

I/he continued more forcibly now, "This *must* be, or there will be an end for all nations. It is in the hands of you brothers. I trust your ears will hear. Take note and reflect within on these words. The minds of you all must change if there is to be survival and an end to suffering. Innocent little children have no desire for fighting, but they learn from their elders. That is what I have come to say. The rest is up to you. I cannot make you follow these words, but the consequences of ignoring them are indeed grave."

A shiver passes through me. I am back as myself in 1991 with

Andreas standing quietly by my side.

"How do you feel?" he looked at me attentively, peering into my face.

Shaken by the experience, I asked, "Was that past or future? Was that really me?"

"It is relevant for all times but particularly for now. The Earth's resources are not so great that they can be wasted on warfare. So much of your planet is in danger of being damaged irreversibly, through actions taken in war and in defense programs. If only that energy could be put to good use. How wonderful that would be. Then too, we are greatly concerned with the damage done to souls."

Andreas watched me closely to see if I understood. He began to pace up and down the room, his glow leaving a trail behind him as he went. "We are anxious, not only about the planet itself, though this is important. We are distressed to see that so much of mankind has lost contact with its intended destiny. In short, man appears to be lost. He cannot seem to find his way, to stop the downward slide into despair and disease that despair brings. Too many have lost hope of ever recovering goodness in the land. Many are trying, but feel they are fighting a losing battle." He stopped pacing to look at me again, to see if my attention was flagging.

Satisfied, he went on, "Let us get a few basic universal laws established in your mind. These laws are unbreakable. They cannot be altered in any way whatsoever, except by the law of grace. Call them what you will. Spiritual laws, Cosmic laws, God's laws, Laws of nature. They are all the same and are immutable.

"It could be said that warfare breaks many laws of life on a horrific scale. It affects large numbers of the population. We cannot state too strongly that where one knowingly and deliberately inflicts injury on another, whether physical, mentally or emotionally, then that injury will return to the instigator *in full*. If only out of self-preservation, the peoples on your planet would do well to keep this in mind. There is much more we could say, but it is time to leave."

The words became fuzzy. He faded in and out of my vision. I was losing the connection. I could not even think. Dimly aware it was all recorded, I slept.

I slept for hours. Dawn was creeping through the gap in the drawn curtains when I awoke. The clock ticked on, indifferent to all that had taken place the night before. It was calm and quiet in my cozy living room, an oasis in the stir of life outside.

I rose stiffly from the armchair, had a good stretch, and padded in my slippers into the kitchen to make a cup of tea. I needed to get things in order in my mind. I knew there was more, much more to come. Andreas was leading me to something. What was he going to introduce next? What did the desert scene mean? There was a hint of our world in need. He referred to the importance of ceasing warfare. If only! How could this ever be? Hadn't there been war on the planet ever since records began? Was it really possible to end the cycle of aggression that seemed to be in man's genes?

As if going back to one past lifetime was not enough, my guidance took me back to a few others. One of these was a most unusual and unexpected experience to a past existence.

I settle down to my inner state and, very soon, am sitting on a bench with my eyes closed, as if dozing. I realize I can hear the murmur of men gossiping and of children shrieking happily as they play somewhere in the playground of a school. I hear the rattle of cartwheels over cobblestones. I open my eyes and see I am in a village market square, framed by ramshackle buildings.

A horse-drawn carriage rumbles noisily out of a side street and across the cobbles. I step aside quickly for the driver did not appear to have seen me as I got up from the bench.

Uncertain what to do, I make my way to a house on the shady side of the square and enter a doorway. I want to ask where I am, but there is nobody about. Facing me are stairs. I climb these to the landing. I tread carefully, feeling and smelling the wood. The floorboards creak as I walk along. A door is opening to a room at the far end. I enter warily, wondering what I will find.

An old woman is laying on a bed against the far wall. In the dim light, I make out several figures standing around. It is clear they are waiting for her to die. Before I can leave the woman on the bed sees me, lifts her arm, and beckons me over. I hesitate, not wanting to intrude. She keeps waving at me, and I go over to her. She looks at me with pale watery eyes. I kneel awkwardly beside her and take her fragile bony hand in mine. She smiles weakly at me. I stroke her brow and bring her hand to my cheek. We stay together like this for some time until at last she closes her eyes in peace. She is gone. The waiting people in the room draw near, completely ignoring me.

I rise and walk slowly from the room. I go down the dusty stairs out into the heat and sunshine of the day. I am confused. Why had the others in the room ignored me? The old woman was real enough and saw me clearly.

I am thirsty now. A dog is waiting by the fountain in the middle of the square. He can see me. "Who was that old woman?" I ask him, knowing he cannot answer.

"She was you" replied a strong male voice from the other side of the fountain. Startled, I peer through the cascading water, where I see a tall figure.

"What do you mean, me? How can she be? Who are you?"

"She was your past and you are her future."

Suddenly, I am returned home. Another journey was over.

I later understood that we say there is no such thing as time and yet we have not really understood that our soul essence, our consciousness can be anywhere and everywhere across time. It is only our current conscious state that prevents such travel and connection. Perhaps this is good, for how would we cope with multi lives all at once. I doubt we would manage without some breakdown. But, and it is a big but, it explains how mediums and psychics can connect with loved ones who have long ago passed on. Even though they may have since re-incarnated into different bodies, they have the same soul and soul memories which never dies. It explains how mediums can connect with loved one's memories in connection with you. It is much easier for them to do this when you are thinking about the loved one. It explains how so many can communicate across time with those such as Jesus, the Angels, and the Masters.

Roy came over and joined me regularly after work. He was able to monitor and explain many new experiences I was having. There was never enough time. Fitting things in grew into a major problem. If the daylight hours were doubled, they still would not be enough.

Dishes still had to be washed, letters had to be written, and housework and the garden attended to. Roy continued to visit, seldom absent, encouraging me and adding his considerable energy to enable communication to be passed through me. I never told him what the dapper medium had said. I would soon be back in the office. My sick leave was nearly over, and time was running out, but there was much more to come.

Chapter 7

Enter Raman

I stared absentmindedly out of the kitchen window, watching blackbirds chase each other across my very English lawn and dreamed of desert scenes. Soon I sensed someone behind me. It was Andreas, standing quietly, observing. Ever the gentleman, I knew he was waiting until I had completed my thinking.

"It is time for your next instruction," he said. "Another will come to you. Do not be surprised when it happens. You will not see quite so much of me, though I will be present if you need me."

My heart sank. Andreas was very dear to me. I did not want anybody else. I did not want him to leave me, the way Janus had.

"It has already been arranged," he said decisively. "Your new teacher is called Raman." More softly now, he said, "I won't be far away."

"Wang Lu will stay, won't he? *He* will still come, won't he?" I could hear the whine in my voice, but I did not care. I did not want to lose everybody.

Andreas looked at me, understanding. "His part was to introduce the healing. He has completed his task. He must now move on."

"Oh." My heart leaden, I felt deserted.

Andreas saw my crestfallen face, took my head in his hands, and kissed me softly on the forehead.

"I will leave you with your thoughts," he said and was gone.

A week dragged by. Nothing happened. Despondent, I wandered aimlessly around the house, feeling let down, abandoned, and miserable. What had I done wrong? Why couldn't I make my connections anymore? The rain drummed on the windowpane as I sat staring into space. Water gushed and splashed along the guttering, spilling over the top. It was not a night to be out. I was glad to be indoors. The clock ticked on, uncaring, measuring time. I sat alone, upright in the chair, with one solitary table lamp casting soft shadows over the furniture and walls. My eyes grew heavy and closed.

"I have come." A gruff voice broke the calm. I nearly fell off my chair with surprise. I did not recognize the voice.

"I have been waiting to come." He sounded aggrieved.

His tone ruffled me. "Well, what stopped you? I have certainly been asking for someone. Who are you anyway?"

"Look and you will see." It was a command, not a request.

I looked and saw before me a tall, thickset full-blown rajah wearing what I could only describe as a white uniform. A dark dense beard hid a solid bull neck. On his head was a white turban with an enormous red jewel in the center. Flashes of light from this shot over his forehead and heavy brows. I could only describe him as bulky, and I would have loved to touch him, but knew this was not possible. His air of authority was unmistakable. I realized I should not be flippant with him as I had been with Janus. He was to be treated with respect. Just as I thought this, he winked.

"Well, well. So you are the one who wants to help and do your bit in the world. They told me you were enthusiastic, not to say impatient," he said gruffly. "You know, child, with knowledge comes responsibility. You are aware of that, are you not? When you have valuable information, you must do something with it. Are you sure you have sufficient application, stamina, and determination?"

"I think so. I will try at least," I said. He was going to be a tough teacher. I was trying hard to come to terms with the fact that even with my eyes shut, I could see and talk to a person who was not alive. I felt I had moved into a different time frame. He seemed real enough to me as I watched him look around for a chair. Finding one, he sat down and spread his long, immaculately clothed legs out before him. He leaned forward, large hands dangling over his knees.

"Let me tell you, child. When I, Raman, was a small boy, I came under the discipline of my peers. I knew that as a child I could always depend on the care and leadership that was ever present. And so as a child, *I* had no fear of being deserted. There was no lack of security. *I* felt content in the knowledge that I would be cared for."

I knew this was a dig at my despondent mood earlier. It is all right for you, I mumbled under my breath. At least you had someone.

The massive figure looked at me sharply, a reprimand in his eyes. "I did not need to concern myself with higher matters, until such time as I too was to take up the reins of leadership, with all the responsibilities that go with it. I am now that one who not only has a position but also a responsibility towards those who look to me for guidance." He paused. "It is not as enviable a position as one might think." He looked at me meaningfully. He smiled wryly. "You ask, why am I telling you this?"

His head went up proudly. He smoothed his already perfect trousers. "These words should be a comfort to you in times of your loneliness, in times when the burden rests heavily on your shoulders."

"What does he know of loneliness?" I muttered to myself. His dark eyes softened with deep understanding. Ashamed of my thoughts, I realized I was being unfair. I acknowledged that never in my whole life had there been a man who cared for me in a protective or responsible way. During the war, the whole family had been separated from my father. When it ended, we grew up, still without him. I missed having a dad around more now that I was much older. I made my mind up there and then. Raman could be the fatherly caring authority I had lacked in my life. I could and would accept him.

"Let us get down to work," he commanded. "We will begin your training. Every man, woman, and child have a need to be loved and to love. That need is in *everyone* on the planet, whether they are kindly souls, thieves, or murderers. Everybody has it within them to be astounding, to be something great. There are *no* exceptions. We must drag up to the light what each is capable of and show them their worth. Let me show you a picture in which you will go down in a lift. Use your mind for this."

I was not expected to argue. A miner's lift cage appeared to my mind. I got in, and rattling as it went, it began to descend, passing several levels until eventually it reached bottom. The metal bar securing the gate clanged as it opened. I got out. Alone, quite alone in the silence and gloom, I walked slowly along the dusty, shored-up passages to a large opening.

Raman's voice commanded: "Look around, child."

Like a child, I obeyed. Everywhere there were glints of gold in the dark face of black rock.

Raman's gravel voice cut into the darkness. "Yes, there are nuggets of gold all around you, waiting to be discovered. They have value and worth. You must find them and bring them to the light. Everyone has the qualities that we are looking for. This is your task."

"But they are so deeply buried and scattered. I could be here forever doing this job," I cried. The prospect was overwhelming. The walls faded slowly, and I was back in Raman's presence.

"Have you understood what is intended?" he asked, arms folded across his chest.

"I think so," I said. I did not want to get it wrong. This was my first test. "I am to help people discover what they are capable of?"

He nodded. "Look! Would you agree that you are able to communicate with me?"

"Yes, it appears that way."

Raman stood up and had a good stretch. I feared he would knock an ornament over. I forgot that he was spirit and might not affect solid objects. Perhaps he gets stiff after sitting so long, I mused. I wondered if a spirit would be able to knock anything over. And did they ever get stiff? I smiled to myself as I realized they must have been stiff at some point when they died. I almost laughed at my own joke when Raman's voice interrupted my straying thoughts.

"So far, you have taken a lot on trust and believed in what we have said."

"Yes, I believe what has happened so far. I did have a head start though."

"Oh? What was that?" His shaggy eyebrows went up in surprise.

I drew a deep breath. "I believe, have always believed that the soul does not die with the physical body. If it does not die, then it lives, like you. If it lives, then what does it do in its new existence? I believe it can reincarnate because I have had my own personal experience to prove it. *I remembered my past life experience as an Arab youth*. But not everyone thinks the same way as I do."

I wished he would sit down again. It cricked even my non-physical neck to look up at him. It was in that instant that I realized wherever I went during these meditations, I felt as real and living and experiencing every bit as much as I did in my physical everyday life. I had entered a different world, a higher dimension. This would be why, when others were present, they could not see my spirit guides as I could. I could not know it then, but this too was to change. In the years ahead, others present would see spirit beings with me.

I learned that whatever dimension you are experiencing it

feels just as real as everyday third dimensional life and those in your experience are as real to you too. You and they can exist in those surroundings as easily as if it were normal.

"Excellent. Good!" Raman continued and was pleased. He stroked his black bushy beard in satisfaction. "You can see the connections now. You can see where we are going."

"Er, not really!" I had lost the thread.

"Think it through. If everyone thought the way you do and believed that what they do in this life would have a consequence for them in their future lives, good or bad, depending on their actions, then they would think about their actions more. They would know they would come to experience consequences of what they put into effect now.

"To put it into simple terms, you get back what you give, good or bad. How are you going to prove to the public that life continues and that what we have just said is valid and has truth?"

"I don't know." I felt inadequate again.

He put a strong hefty arm across my shoulders. "Come, come, child! You have been receiving training, have you not? You can communicate, not only with us but also with other minds no longer in physical form. We are well aware that people are skeptical about your kind of activity and that you have kept very quiet about it so far, especially about your communication with us."

I thought of my youngest son and how he was a lay preacher as a born-again Christian. I would be an embarrassment to him, to say the least. He would say it was the work of the devil. I loved him and knew it could create a rift in the family if I said too much. I shifted uncomfortably under the weight of Raman's arm. I recognized a buildup when I saw it.

"We are asking you to open your mouth regarding your beliefs and findings. To be more specific, and to begin with, you are to open a development group. Start a training program to help the rediscovery and use of the inner senses that all possess. So many individuals have lost the ability though nonuse. These can easily be brought into action again, with direction. When this has been accomplished, then contact may be made with their own inner selves, their soul selves. This will give them a great advantage. They will discover their own worth. Do not be afraid to approach people. There will of course be one or two who are so unaccustomed to having interest shown in them that they will not know how to react. Your approach will become easier with practice. Seek to be in environments where it is acceptable to approach complete strangers, such as at conferences and talks. It is more acceptable this way. It will get easier with practice. Do not become a hermit. Will you help?"

"Oh, my goodness! How can I?" I sighed miserably. "I could go to more lectures, I suppose."

Ignoring my comment, Raman continued, "Each person possesses a mental, a physical, and a soul consciousness, that is, mind, body and soul. The mental speaks for itself and is fed day to day with stimulation of mind activity, such as reading, watching television, interacting with others, making conscious decisions, etc.

"The physical consciousness or subconscious is the one that takes care of your bodily functions. This too is fed. It takes care of your breathing, digestion, responding to invasion of germs, and so on. It does this automatically without you being aware of it, for the most part. However, it also responds to what you tell it. For example, if you are chilly or in contact with someone's cold, you are likely to tell yourself you are bound to get a cold and so you do. Your unconscious mind is programmed to respond to your thoughts. It makes what you tell it a reality."

I remembered how Mary broke her arm and how Jane became paralyzed, all because of their self-talk. I shuddered at the thought. How many times had I said I would give my right arm for a cup of tea? I would be more careful in future.

Raman was still speaking. "The soul/spirit consciousness has been with you since you began existence and works for you for your benefit. It will never go against you. Therefore, if you were able to communicate with it, you could receive an enormous amount of help. You could transform your life into one of happiness and serenity. You could direct your life in the way that is best for you. You could create your reality."

I reflected that was what I was doing now. He was interrupted in his flow by a crash of bins outside in the street. A cat or fox perhaps!

"You see, life goes on," he said dryly. "The object of the training is to bring into the conscious mind what the soul mind is trying to tell it, for its benefit. When this has been accomplished, the soul can then inform you about the other areas of existence. It can pass on communication from beings such as me, who are trying to assist mankind. It can connect with the angelic realm and the masters. All have the ability. It is only a question of application and training." I was quick to notice the reference to training again. He is not as subtle as he thinks he is, I reflected.

"There will come a time in the future when practically all people will use their inner awareness to a greater extent. The time will come when it will be normal to communicate in this way. The odd ones out will be those who have not learnt to benefit from this soul contact. Training is the first step." He paused. "Shall I go on?"

You will anyway, I thought. Aloud, I said, "Yes, please." I wanted to know how this was going to come about. He obviously had a plan.

He turned and wandered round the room, an impressive burly figure, looking at my books lining the walls, as Andreas had. He ran his hands over them, big, powerful, heavy hands.

"We have told you that we are concerned about the planet and the souls of man. We do not have much time to prepare man for events to come, only some of which are a direct consequence of misuse of the earth and nature. We are training others like you to pass on the knowledge, so that a network of understanding is spread across the globe."

"It sounds like big stuff," I commented drily.

"Do we have your agreement? Will you begin a training program for others as we ask? We will be with you, guiding you and communicating with you as you progress. We cannot impose our will on you. You have the right to refuse, to ignore, or even to disbelieve all we have said."

I gulped and stuttered. "But I—I thought I was still in training myself."

"That will continue of course," he said, soothing me with a smile. "Earlier you made a pledge to help humanity."

I had, of course. He was right. Fifteen years ago, I had done just that. I was in Italy on a social visit when, during a perfectly normal conversation, out of my mouth, without me intending to speak, came the words. "I know why I am here on this planet. I am here to help the world when there is a need." I felt stupid and embarrassed saying such a thing and covered it up as much as I could. They were now taking me up on those words.

Many years later I came to know and experience what he meant about other worlds, other existences, and other intelligences. I was not ready for that now.

Chapter 8

A Lifestyle Change

> The burden of suffering seems a tombstone hung about our necks, while in reality it is only the weight which is necessary to keep down the diver while he is hunting for pearls. *Richter*

I tossed and turned that night, unable to sleep. Eventually I gave up on the struggle and went downstairs. "Time to make contact," I mumbled to myself as I plumped up the cushions in my favorite armchair. I sat on and on and on. Nothing happened! Absolutely nothing! I must be stupid. What a waste of time, I thought. Maybe this was telling me I had to keep my feet on the ground, stay balanced, and be sensible.

Two weeks later, a medium told me, "You will be out of your job around spring next year. You have more important work to do." Were they ganging up on me? I wondered. I did not intend to leave and dug my heels in. After all I grumbled, *they* would not pay the bills, would they?

One morning soon after that, I was gripped with stomach pain so bad that I went to the doctor. Before I could say Jack Robinson, I was back on the operating table. The pattern of last year had repeated itself, giving me three months off work. If *they* thought that would make me leave my job, they had another think coming. But I should have known them better. During a meditation before going to hospital, *they* told me that they would use the opportunity. Rightly or wrongly, I immediately took this to mean that I might have a near-death experience. I looked forward to this with excitement since I had heard that it frequently opened avenues of spiritual and psychic contact that could normally take years.

On coming out of the anesthetic, I knew that something had happened, but I did not know what. Roy told me that I had nearly "gone" during the operation. However, the doctors said nothing, and I remembered nothing. I felt cheated and knew without doubt that I had been somewhere. I also felt an extreme nostalgic sadness for the blue star that I could see out of the hospital window. That was my true home.

I lay in my hospital bed, wishing I were elsewhere. The ward was quiet. It was night. I listened to the occasional snuffle and gentle snoring from the other patients. A dull glow from the ward sister's desk down the passage reminded me that at least one other person was awake. I could not sleep despite having had a sleeping pill. My eyes were wide open as I lay thinking about Raman, the Rajah. I remembered the beam of light from the jewel in his headdress. As if in answer to my thoughts, the sturdy figure of Raman took shape before me.

He put his finger to his lips. "Shush!" he said knowing that nobody could see or hear him even if they were wide awake. It was I who had to be quiet. He looked splendid standing there by the bed in his white tunic and leggings. I almost wished he could be seen. I was proud of him, so proud. I painfully eased my body up, careful not to dislodge the tubes and pieces fixed to me.

I lay awake in my hospital bed thinking, my thoughts churning round and round. Was I going mad—sensible, practical me? I still felt quite normal, and after all, everything that had happened so far had given me new zest for life and new happiness, so it could not be bad. Then I remembered the truly uplifting experience with a Divine source that had left me aglow for a week. No, I was *not* imagining all this, I decided. I relaxed and drifted off to sleep at last, just as the day nursing staff arrived with the morning light to wake everyone up.

I was soon home again. The frost on the ground outside sparkled in the early weak sunshine. Roy came to see me. He sat at the dining table, chewing on his pencil.

"Have you thought about giving up your job?" he said.

"Not a chance. It is no good me even thinking about it. I wouldn't have enough money to live on without working," I declared. I was lucky to have so many friends supporting me when I needed it. I was grateful to them and to Roy and knew I should not complain about anything in my life. Even so, it would be good to be in the office chatting to the girls again after my convalescence. I did not like being lonely, I decided.

A little later, when I had returned to work, I was asked to go to the personnel department. It was sympathetically explained to me that several people were to be made redundant. They were sorry, but I was one of those. I was shattered. My world was turned upside down and my security lost, and to a Cancerian, security is everything.

"How long before you draw a pension?" asked Julie, the practical one.

"This is what you get for mixing with all that spooky stuff." Cynthia sniffed. "I said no good would come of it."

That evening, I sat asking for my invisible friends to come to me. I tried hard. Nobody came. I was sure the redundancy had been arranged by them and decided they were avoiding me, waiting for me to adjust to the idea.

I tried again next morning. It was Saturday, and I had plenty of time. Rain was drumming down outside, matching my mood. "Everything is falling on my head," I moaned, wallowing in self-pity.

A familiar glow began to take shape. It was Andreas, the kind and gentle soul.

"Good morning," he said in a soft low voice. His smile was almost apologetic.

I smiled back. "It's all right, Andreas," I told him wearily. "I'm quite resigned to the idea of leaving work, and having to struggle with the bills," I added sarcastically.

He sighed with relief and ignored the inference. He sat down comfortably on a stool and faced me with a steady look from his blue eyes. "We are going to introduce you to more of our team. We have to wait until the planets are in the most favorable alignment, but I will be there when the time is right," he said before departing. It all sounded very mysterious, and I was disappointed with such a brief visit.

I decided I would prepare for the time ahead when I would be without a steady income. I was going to take charge of my life once more. By this time, I had already been in development circles run by local spiritualist churches and had excellent training from them, as well as from Roy. I would begin to hold my own development groups in the evening. In the readings I had had from mediums, they had always said I should do this. It was time to give it a try. If it wasn't meant to work, the groups would collapse, and nobody would come.

Chapter 9

Discovering Nuggets of Gold

Whenever you meet new opportunities, grasp them with both hands. Don't let them go. Utilise all the forces for good that dwell within you and direct them towards these new openings. They will surely flourish and grow. The effect of this growth will spread outwards. *The Little owl Cards*

Over the next few days, I worked out a training curriculum for a full year. I circulated the program that was to run weekly. Despite there being no internet, no personal computers, just word processors and no mobile phones, all went well. The word was passed on and I began teaching. True to his word, Raman was always there in the background, guiding and encouraging. Other guides arrived to help. One was Chin Nee, who much later I discovered was Sechem who insisted I write the latest trilogy of books *Calling Earth* and who is one of the main characters in those books. He frequently interrupted the evening, making suggestions to do this or that. It was always to our benefit. I also learnt that he and I had lives together as far back as Genesis. You can read this in Genesis 34. You could say I fell in love with him all over again, reminding me that true love never dies. Even today he reacts to every emotion and experience I am having. This might explain why when someone has a drawing of a guide there is a strong attachment between them.

Life went on, and the months passed quickly. I learned as much as the students. Those attending each week discovered abilities they never guessed they had. Often they would say that they could never do this or that, only to discover not only that they could, but also that they were excellent at whatever it was they attempted. They were delighted to discover that they too could bring back helpful information from within their meditations. Several of those attending have now gone on to conduct their own circles and development programs for others. To make sure this happened, as soon as I knew I could not teach them more, and they had mastered what they needed I closed the circle. This forced them to move on, to either continue the work in their own circles or move to groups where they could learn what I was not able to teach. I then opened a new circle with fresh people. It did not always work the way I intended and as time went on I ended up running groups for three different levels of ability.

People came, many through direction given in readings, others hearing of the results, and soon I had a waiting list. My living room was crammed with chairs every week. I had to move the television out to make more room. Neighbors wondered why there were so many cars outside on Tuesday evenings. Beyond is an unknown, due to possible restrictions of movement between people due to the virus.

I include here an abbreviated comment made by one who attended a Soul Reading session in my home.

"*I am writing to describe an extraordinary experience that I had when attending a soul reading with Shirley Battie. I and two others were in the room. Shirley's face would change, and other faces would be superimposed on hers. Suddenly Shirley's head disappeared entirely to be replaced with a beautiful blue/purple flame which danced around where her head should have been for at least a minute. I was utterly amazed to see this – I have never seen anything like it before or since – and I was completely sober I can assure you! I was so delighted and astonished that I kept pointing it out to the other two people. If anyone should doubt Shirley's gifts I believe this is real proof of her connection to Spirit. To this day I sometimes wonder if I dreamed this but know I didn't and have the tape from the session with me commenting with astonishment and delight as evidence." Alice*

Word got around, mainly through Roy's contacts, and soon we had a little regular group that came to the channeling on a Friday. Some of these are still with me today after more than thirty years. They came ready to ask questions of the entities that presented themselves. One lady called Ann Pedlar was a regular visitor. Sadly for us, she has left this world now. She could see perfectly well the spirit beings present in the room. She had a wonderful time describing each and every one of them.

"Oh, this is better than the theatre," she exclaimed more than once.

I never knew what or who would come through me. I had no idea what the subject matter would be. All I had to do was to describe the scene I was in, or to describe the being who presented himself, and it took off from there. Today, the spirit beings come into me and can be seen by some of the people present in the room. Not all can see this. The information was often driven by the questions that were posed by those attending.

It was then that I received my next instruction.

"We would like you to learn public speaking," Andreas said one morning. Then he left abruptly.

Well, I had got over my shyness while teaching English to top men in nuclear physics in Italy, but I argued with myself that was not the same. That morning, a brochure dropped through the letterbox. Picking it up, I saw it was from the local council's adult education program. It fell open at the section outlined Public Speaking Course. They might just as well have dropped a brick. This was hardly a hint. By this time, I knew that my guides usually got their way even if it took a long time. I remembered how persistent the nightly writing in Italy was and how it had taken two years before I took notice and began to learn how to write.

I signed up for the seven-week course, during which I was entered for the London Academy of Music and Dramatic Art examination for speaking in public. As I sat in the corridor waiting my turn, I was handed a sealed envelope containing a long list of subjects that we the candidates could choose from to speak on for five minutes. There were many subjects listed, such as the Cottage Industry, the French Revolution, and so on, but heading the list was Psychic Phenomena. I rather think my spirit friends had a hand in it, for it was that that got me through. I passed.

To get practice, I joined the East Dorset Speakers Club, which is the equivalent of the Toastmasters in America and Australia. I gave my first talk at the Friends Meeting House in Bournemouth, Dorset, for the Wessex Research Group, and spoke on how to communicate with guides, teachers, and one's soul. I am sure everyone could hear my knees knocking and it was clear to all how nervous I was. I do not think I did a good job, but it was a start, and I thank the organizer Pat Law, who trusted me enough to let me speak. It was a beginning, and I went on to talk at the Positive Living Group in Bournemouth, run by Angela Underwood, now living in Spain. The Positive Living Groups are still very active and are using Zoom during lockdown. (2021)

Much later, I was to talk all over the world, but thankfully, I did not know what was ahead.

Chapter 10

Double-Edged Sword

How can I sleep when I know the world awaits?
How can I dream when I know the world expects?
What can I do to change the way?
What can I say to make an effect
on this earth of ours on which we stay?

Dear child of mine, you take your heart
and offer it to all who need.
Dear breath from God, you give your soul to love, in life.
Sweetness of light, you sacrifice yourself to show you care.
In this you will show the way that all will see and share.
The Little Owl cards *from the White Brotherhood*

It was 1994 and I was short of time once more. I eased up on the meditations. There were days when I did not meditate at all. I began to panic. Lack of money worried me. Despite good intentions, these concerns took precedence over communicating with spirits, who were not able to produce money out of a hat, no matter how clever they were. I knew I would never return to my former complacency. I would never again be able to detach myself from others around me or ignore what was happening in the world. Touched and affected by everything, I found myself weeping over atrocities happening everywhere in the world. I desperately wanted to end the appalling suffering. But what could one person meditating alone do that would make any difference? One part of me struggled to live the life of sublime ignorance I'd had before I began the communications, but a greater part of me insisted I could never again be the same.

As if in answer to my despondency, Andreas came yet again, glowing softly.

"Do not be sad," he said gently. "Have you forgotten there is a plan? Did we not tell you that man is to see a better life?"

"People are so brave in their suffering," I said, fighting back tears. "I'm suffering inside with them, yet I do nothing."

"It is the price you pay for becoming sensitive," Andreas replied. "Do you think that we do not weep?" he asked quietly. "Do you think that we do not feel anger when we see injustice? When you become part of the whole, you feel acutely all that is contained there. You cannot remain impervious to happenings in the creation."

I looked at him wonderingly. He seemed so calm, always so peaceful. I could not picture him being angry.

Andreas returned my gaze. "Man's inhumanity has to cease, for he is destroying his own soul by his conduct. Power, greed, envy, and fear—all these things need to be converted to love. Show by example. It *can* be done.

"We do understand your need to attend to your material life, you know."

I should have known he was aware of my wild swings between wanting to do something and wanting to go back to doing nothing but attend exclusively to my own life.

I saw his blue eyes brighten as if he wanted to encourage me. "You know, no meditative sitting is wasted, even if the duration is only for two minutes. Even if you receive no profound truths, no connection is ever lost. The touching of two contact points is sufficient to create a spark. When an electrician connects two wires even for a second, contact is made. It is important for us to test the circuit and maintain the connection. We are content when we are assured that the contact points are clean and ready at any moment. But it is necessary for you to make the required effort. A finger on the doorbell is sufficient to bring somebody to the door."

"I'm afraid I won't be adequate for the job you seem to have in mind," I said.

Andreas pondered on this. I knew he was picking his words carefully. "Do you truly believe that we are all trying to help man and the planet?"

"Yes," I said, my voice scarcely above a whisper.

"Do you truly believe that there is a greater intelligence than yours or mine and that the souls of men continue after physical death?"

"Yes," I said again.

"Let me assure you that every single thing you do, think, or say has an effect. Teach others to concentrate their thoughts towards betterment of world conditions and men's minds. The energies that are concentrated into these thoughts have a powerful effect. When you apply yourselves in this positive way, we support you with greater energies, making the impact even more effective. You might say that we rejoice and rush to assist when man uses his will to help others. We cannot alter man's freedom to act one way or the other, for that is against the Law, but we can support and encourage his actions when they are for the benefit of all. Continue to teach what is in your heart, and we will support and guide you. We have told you this before. Why are you so afraid?"

I blinked back tears, twisting my hands in my lap. "Because you have implied there is a lot more to come and I don't know if I will come up to scratch."

"Why don't you take one step at a time and deal with what you have at the moment? You know, when you are doubtful, we must step back and allow you time to make up your own mind, without influence from us. You then get the mistaken idea that you have been abandoned. This can make you feel desolate and unhappy, causing you to run off to a medium or someone else for assurance, when the only true conviction should come from within yourself." He took my hands in his, stilling them.

His eyes told me that he knew all my thoughts. He was so right in what he had said.

"You want to know how you can help ease the pain and suffering?"

"Yes. I feel I am a hypocrite. I say I want to do something and yet do nothing," I confessed. "I'm ashamed I don't do more."

He smiled with that amazing look. "Hold the light simply by being the best that you can be in helping others, have good feelings for others and do not allow fear. When retaining the light, dark energies cannot enter. As we have said before, if you are of the light vibration the dark will destroy itself if it tries to come in, because it would be uncomfortable, simply like putting a weak fuse into a strong current. Providing you hold the light by being the best you can be then nothing can hurt you."

I wondered if I had enough light in me to make a difference.

Andreas realised he needed to reassure me for he said, "The dark forces cannot have a footing in this world. They cannot sustain themselves in the light that is being shown all over. They cannot endure in the light that is shown by all loving creatures, and the human race and beings of all kinds. The dark powers have no standing in this light. They cannot endure it. They will either leave or change until they can endure and be part of the light. It will be as it is meant to be. But have no fear of the dark powers at any time while we continue to be as we are, wonderful, wonderful beings of light."

What am I still learning in this situation that we are all in? I have learnt and am in awe of people and have seen how wonderful they are, how kind and caring they are. I have witnessed absolute kindness and gentleness in all those I have come across. I am in awe in how they are dealing with this difficult period. I am grateful for my own position, where I live, and am aware that others are not so happily placed. I can only speak of those I see around me; I cannot speak for others. But where there are pockets where people are kind, generous and loving to all those around them I am grateful and am heartened as a human. I am in awe of how they deal with what they are faced with. I will never ever take for granted my own position in life. I am in awe of others. They are wonderful.

Andreas went on, "We are asking you to think in wider terms—global terms. We are asking you to make known what we teach you.

"Re the global situation. You are all in this together, but so many are not quite so capable of saying what they wish to say. All races, all colours, all genders, are all in this together. You need to remember that you are all one family on your home planet Earth. This situation should unite you as one for you are all in the same boat, all of you, whether you are enjoying it or whether you are absolutely hating it, whether you are in pain or in love. You are all in this together. The outcome will be according to whether you unite with each other and whether you love each other. Or will you continue the pattern of fighting one with the other? Will you continue the pattern of one war after the other in one country after the other until there is nothing left but tragedy and destruction? If you are fortunate in living reasonable lives, may you remember that you are all one together on the same planet. Maybe, each of you, will suffer what you did not expect to suffer, or you may sail through. Look to your heart, look to the sense of unity that this situation has brought upon the entire planet and see that this can be a uniting force.

"The biggest difficulty mankind has is not being able to forgive. Men in many countries continue to keep alive the memories of vile deeds inflicted upon them. They nurture and feed the pain they hold in their hearts. The hate this engenders eats at them and continues to ruin their lives. What they do not realize is that unless this hate is dispelled from them, it will continue to be a part of them even into their future lives. What they do not realize is that they are not alone in holding on to these destructive forces. This being so, on reincarnating they will certainly meet others like themselves, for like attracts like. They will then either combine forces to attack others and become that which they hated in their former life, or they will attack each other. Either way they will have become victims of their own past hatred.

"We say to these poor unfortunate souls, 'Love those who do not appear to deserve it. Until compassion and understanding is shown to those who have done wrong, neither one can be helped. These wrongdoers may have begun as innocent victims themselves, holding on to a memory of pain, as many are doing. We plead with you to break the chain of hate. Even if it is an effort, try to think kindly, with compassion and pity."

He released my hands and walked around the room. I noticed his tread made no sound. In the street outside, I heard a cat crying like a baby. Andreas came back to where I sat in the corner.

"If you can understand what I have said, then you can explain it to others. You *will* come across those who consider themselves victims, injured by others. Help them to feel compassion, because one who has committed unforgivable acts is destined to feel the painful consequences in future life. If only they could realize how much they would benefit from this understanding." Andreas sat down and folded his arms.

I realized I had been given a lesson. It dawned on me that he did not come unless I asked for help, even if that request was only in my mind, as a need. If I could only be like Andreas, I would be happy.

He broke into my thoughts gently. "My dear child, do you think I was always this way? You can be like me and more if you wish it. There is time."

"Time goes so fast," I said.

"Hmm! We will see what we can arrange. There is to be a milestone in your program," he added with enthusiasm. "I will leave you now to think over what I have said." With that, Andreas my glowing one was gone, leaving me alone with my thoughts.

I sat very still in the quiet room. I watched the shadows created by the flickering candle and thought over my life. Were there any areas in my past where I had to forgive? Or perhaps it was I who needed to be forgiven.

Chapter 11

Physical Journeys

Oh yet we trust that somehow good
will be the final goal of ill.
But what am I?
An infant crying in the night:
an infant crying for the light:
and with no language but a cry.
Tennyson

The time to leave my job arrived at last. With care, I had managed to pay the bills because I had saved in preparation for this time. I had downsized my house at the time of my divorce to keep me going and out of debt. I had also saved a little in the bank against a rainy day. Well, this was the rainy day for sure.

The benefits were that I had more free time, and this was when my guides hotted things up for me. For one thing, it took hours every day to transcribe the tapes on what would nowadays be considered an archaic typewriter. I used a word processor but thank goodness for computers that we have now. I still have boxes and boxes of cassette tapes of recorded channelled information given by spirit. Unfortunately even cassette tapes are redundant now and so what I have may well be jettisoned when I too pass on.

French Pyrenees

It was not long before my spirit friends demonstrated how much they organized and set things up in advance. All would go well, providing I noticed and followed through with the little suggestions they gave me. I call these my threads which I must follow. I was no longer in paid employment; my time was my own, or I should say, theirs.

As always, it was during a meditation that I was able to hear their words.

"We would like you to go to the French Pyrenees," they said. And as usual, I did not know the reason. I had not learned to ask for more information as I do now. I needed no second bidding to go. During my previous time spent working in France, I learned to love the French Pyrenees. I was more than happy to return there. Roy was to accompany me.

We had a great time touring. At each stop, Roy would give a reading to any who wanted one. I would translate it into French. Our destination was Cathar country, and we naturally gravitated towards Rennes-le-Château and Rennes-les-Bains. Sitting on the bank of a river watching the water rush by, I was suddenly back in time, living as a youth called Jean Luc. I knew my home had been there.

This was just passing interest until we stopped at Rennes-le-Château, intending to visit the famous church written about in *The Bible Code* and other books. Irrationally, I felt extreme unease and was mightily relieved when we discovered the church was closed and that we would have to come back at another time. I drove away relieved and happier now and we continued our tour.

A day or two later, we pulled into a little country lay-by to buy some fruit from a barrow. Roy went off to get the fruit, and I stayed by the car. Into the same lay-by came a coach. I watched as the passengers poured off with the same intention of buying fruit. Like me, some stayed close by the vehicles and took the advantage of getting some air. I got into conversation, when to our mutual delight I discovered this was a coachload of mediums, healers, and therapists from Holland. The chance of this happening was more than coincidence, and I felt my spirit helpers had a hand in this meeting. Sure enough, some days later, we bumped into them again and had a joint venture to do with the Cathar connection. As a result of our meeting I was later invited to Holland to give readings and a talk. Spirit always has it in hand when they have a plan.

On our way home, Roy was determined to visit Rennes-le-Château, and so once more, I drove up the mountain. This time to my dismay the church was open. At the entrance of the church is a stone statue of a devil that is holding the stoup, which is a basin for holding holy water. He is Asmodeus, the limping devil who guards King Solomon's temple. Statues of angels are on a pedestal, on which are carved two griffons, treasure keepers. At the time I was unaware of the history of this place or the legend of the Holy Grail surrounding it. I could not understand my reluctance as I went into the church. As soon as I stepped inside, I smelled the terrible stench of death. My legs trembled so violently I thought I would collapse. I fled from that awful place and sat outside on a bench. I wept uncontrollable, terrible floods of tears. I could not stop.

Roy came out and found me in my distressed state. "Clearly, this is why we've been asked to come," he said. "You must go back in. You cannot ignore this one."

He could be very firm when he wanted to. With great trepidation and shaking legs, I went back inside. In a pew, I knelt and prayed for help. I prayed for the good and the bad. As soon as I did this, I knew without doubt what had happened years before. I was told that my name was Jean Luc and that I had been walled up alive in that church. Those who had done this were now trapped themselves. I was to release them and did so with my prayers.

The moment it was done, I felt an enormous change in the church, and I no longer suffered the earlier dreadful sensations. It was over. It was done. On leaving, I saw above the gate to the churchyard the words *Cette Place et Terrible.*

But the Cathar connection was not done with us yet. I was driving along with Roy when suddenly and without warning I veered sharply up a side road. It felt as if someone had taken control of the car. This took us to a car park from which was the start of a climb on foot to a high Cathar stronghold castle, Puilaurens. After a hot climb up a zigzag path, we arrived at the summit. Once there inside the castle ruins, Roy went into a trance and was taken back to a former time as a Cathar female, giving many details of life.

PUILAURENS

During our tour, I walked into a shop-cum-restaurant. The lady behind the counter stared at me as I entered. "You are a Cathar," she stated bluntly as if it was the most normal thing to say to a stranger. So ended our Cathar experience.

New Mexico

The second request from spirit to travel came in June 1994 while I was in Maryland near Washington DC. "We need you to go to New Mexico," they said.

This time I asked why, and of course they did not tell me. It would be the first time I had gone abroad on my own just for a holiday and not for work. I just knew I had to go. I browsed through the brochures and booked a tour. I had an idea the suggestion to go to New Mexico was to do with Native Americans because an Indian guide, Joe, was giving me so many dance rituals and messages that I could not ignore him. He told me I had to learn what they meant. I should explain that Indian Joe was really Roy's guide and White Owl was mine. Neither makes any appearances anymore. I have come to realize that guides are with us to teach us along certain parts of our journey, and when we have come through those parts, they hand us over to other guides for the next stage. This would also explain why many psychics and mediums have several guide drawings and not just one.

I took them up on the suggestion to go to New Mexico. The plane flew to El Paso, where I joined the tour group. Right from the start, I knew I had made the right choice with Tauck Tours as tour operator. It was and still is the best coach tour I have ever experienced. The days passed visiting this area and that with many highlights. However, I had no idea what I was to do, or when I was to do it regarding my guide's purpose in sending me.

I did not do much in the way of meditating either since we were on the road early or arrived late each day.

The tour was drawing to a close with Santa Fe as our stop for three days, giving me time to shop and explore. We were staying at the Inn of the Mountain Gods, which I thought was a most delightful name. It was the last day there and as I had had no real time to browse so I decided to give one of the organized excursions a miss. As I wandered into a shop, the lady behind the counter looked up at me, stating firmly, “You read palms. Read mine.”

“How did you know?” I asked in surprise.

“I saw it as soon as you came in.”

That should have told me something, but I read her hands anyway. She burst into tears. It seemed I was hitting the right buttons. The assistant wanted her hands read too. It did not take long before she was crying as well. This is good, I thought, walking into shops and making people cry. The upshot was that Lynda, the owner, asked me if I would give her a reading after she finished work. This meant I would miss the farewell to Santa Fe meal the tour had organized, and they were always good.

Reluctantly, I agreed, thinking perhaps this could be why spirit wanted me there. Lynda came to my hotel room at the proposed time. I gave her a reading, none of which I can remember now. She then surprised me by offering to give me a reading in return. I had not expected this but happily accepted. She went into deep trance and for over an hour gave me precise instructions on what I was to do the following day. It was a Native American who spoke through her.

The tour was planned to visit Taos next, an original Indian village. My instructions from the American Indian were that I was not to speak of my purpose to anybody during my journey on the coach, and to be silent. This proved to be difficult since the lady next to me was a lovely Jewish lady from New York who wanted to talk almost nonstop. I was not to take any photographs, and I was not to do any shopping. This was a bit of a blow since Taos is a tourist place with lots of opportunities for both.

I had to find a place in the village where nobody was around. That will be a good trick, I thought, since there would be coach-loads arriving all the time and the place would be swarming with tourists.

"We will place a pyramid over you that nobody will enter," the spirit guide said. I would be told what I was to do when I had found the right spot. Arriving at Taos, I told the coach driver Daniel and tour guide Lane not to worry about me if I disappeared from the group.

Daniel must have guessed since he gave me the thumbs-up sign and said, "Good luck."

After a little wander round, I found a place in the back lanes and listened in. I was told I was to be a transmitter and work in multiple levels and was preparing the way for new babies to come. I was instructed to bring down from the mountains the spiritual energies that the present modern-day Native Americans were in danger of losing. It was all beyond my understanding in many ways, but true to their words, there was not a soul in sight during the whole time. The disembodied voice told me exactly what to do. This was a miracle for I was there a good half hour. I wondered if what I did made any difference because I have no way of knowing. Perhaps it was simply a test to see if I would follow instructions, for there was more to come. As a footnote, I suspect that Taos is no longer as it was in 1994 and has grown enormously since then if the current Web site is anything to go by.

Borneo

It was in 1996 when my lovely spirit guides asked if I would go to Borneo. I realised that at 62 years of age if I had any sense I would go with a tour and not go alone. As usual I had no idea why I was needed there or what I would do when there. The tour took us to a former Japanese prison camp where terrible things had happened. I was wandering around on my own when very suddenly two enormous angels stood on either side of me. I was told telepathically to forgive both the prisoners and the Japanese guards and release the land of the dreadful things that had occurred. The land was to be cleared of those energies.

Once again I was reminded that spirit or angels cannot or will not do this for us and it is for those incarnated to do so if we are to evolve into a higher state. The angels were there to protect me from the dark energies as they were being released.

I did not know it then but the sites we visited in New Mexico such as White Sands Missile testing centre, Alamogordo, Roswell and Carlsbad had so much more to do with my contact with space beings that came later. I was to visit America many more times on instruction from my guides. Spirit had it all in hand.

It was time to go home and get on with my life, but I will never forget New Mexico and truly hope to be able to return. I loved Santa Fe and the desert. My first journey abroad alone was a huge success in building my confidence.

Florida

More proof on how my spirit friends set things in motion by putting me in the most unlikely places. I received an invitation to go to Gainesville in Florida, give readings and to give a talk. As usual I accepted. What I did not know was that the talk was to take place in a large hall in the Bible belt. Was this a test?

"I don't know if anyone will come," my host said but we

will see. It was not encouraging but I knew nothing happens by chance. I cannot even remember what the talk was about now. All I remember were the large numbers pouring in through the doors. People had to find room by sitting in the aisles and along the walls. People were still arriving when we had to shut the doors as there was simply no more room. Everyone there was attentive and most of all I was not heckled at all.

Was this a set up by my spirit friends, to get information that was denied to so many because of strict religious rules? I do not know. But for sure the minds were opened and I did not hold back.

I have returned several times to work in other parts of Florida and have enjoyed my time there immensely. It all began in Minneapolis but that is another long story.

Brazil 1999

Evidence of new arrangements came soon. I was in Seattle for a month, working. I had given myself two weeks free of work when I arranged flights. I thought that if there wasn't sufficient work to cover that, I would give myself a holiday and go to see the Grand Canyon.

What happened instead was a message from my spirit friends. "We want you to go to a village in Brazil," they said.

"Fine," I replied. "When I have learnt Portuguese."

"We want you to go now."

Fortunately, I had read a book about the village they named when I was in Australia but had no intention of visiting. I asked my helpers many questions regarding this request until they persuaded me sufficiently that it was important that I go and that I go immediately. Timing was important. So much for my holiday to the Grand Canyon! I booked a flight and bought a Portuguese/English dictionary at the airport. It was my first time in Brazil, and it was not the easiest journey to get to the village.

However, I had a fabulous time once I arrived after a three hour coach drive from Brazilia. What was most odd was that on my first day there, when I explained to an interpreter the reason for my visit, he had himself been given the same information and understood the role I had to play. The timing was important in more ways than one but there is too much to be included in this book. It was not to be my only visit to the village. I knew I had to go back, and later at home, I asked my spirit friends when.

It was now 2000. Once more the timing was precise. "We want you to get a crystal sword," they said, "and take it to the village in Brazil this October."

Somehow I managed to get one made for me in Glastonbury, just in time. It was to be needed, and if I had known just how much, I might not have gone on the second journey. It had been arranged for me to work for two weeks in a spiritual center in São Paulo after my stay in the village. I was to contact a certain man in charge for details, and I would stay with a lady who spoke English.

The energies were so different in the village from the first visit that it depressed and saddened me. I meditated on it as soon as I could. I had written to book accommodation to a pousada I had seen during my first visit. I received no reply but I went anyway, hoping it would be alright. I discovered when I finally got there that the healer they called Joao de Deus had forbidden the postman to deliver any mail from abroad to pousadas that he had no control over. He was taking backhanders from most pousadas. I also discovered that he had forbidden the owner of the pousada I was staying to take me anywhere he did not allow. The owner, a beautiful soul said if he disobeyed, he would be thrown out of the village.

During my visits to this village I was invited to attend a special Daime ceremony involving the taking of ayahuasca. Brazilian natives had come in order to prepare the brew. I survived both ceremonies even though I was unprepared for it all. I am still alive. But also during these events I met a gorgeous man called Lucio who showered me with rather amorous kisses each time we met. I declined his plea to stay with him.

While there a small family group arrived at the pousada. Among the group was a beautiful young girl who was not able to speak at all. They had taken her to doctors, but nothing could be done for her. I offered healing although I knew it would be forbidden by Joao if he found out. During the healing I was told by spirit to tell her that she would speak within two weeks. They returned a week later, kissing and hugging me, delighted that she was able to talk.

Yet another was a young woman who asked me for healing. I tuned in and was told that her heart was bleeding for a lost love and the bottom had dropped out of her world. It was exactly right for she told me later that there was a problem with her heart and her lower regions. Amazing how the body takes on the emotional distress and produces a physical aliment to match. There was much I could write about what went on while I was at the village, but this book is not the place to say more.

My guides said, "You will need the sword to change the energies. Face everything with trust. You are strong enough to keep safe." It was explained to me how to use the sword as I walked around the area. The words to me came strongly.

"LOTS OF WORK—CHALLENGES—FIGHTING AND CHANGING DARK ENERGIES—NEED PROTECTION AND HELP—NEED HELP FROM GUIDES AND THOSE OF THE LIGHT—INTO HEAVY STUFF HERE."

I doubted my ability to deal with this, but I was told to write.

This is what came from my spirit friends: *"You are in the right place. The reasons are yet to be seen. Hold on and trust in us. We have never let you down or used you falsely. You know this to be so. Your work is not always to be one of joy, and you will be taken as before into the dark places. Shine in these areas. Do not allow the darkness to overwhelm you. The brothers of the dark will not submerse your soul. Fear not. Trust and love. You have our blessing. Be calm, regain your serenity."*

I later learned that black magic was flourishing in that place, and this was what I was fighting. I do not want to do that too often, that is for sure. Out of consideration for the village I will not name it, but I have learned that the source of the dark and evil energies has now been removed. I pray that the village has been cleared of those dark energies but I have not been back since.

While I was there, the village had what is called the Day of the Dead, when families get together and visit the graves of relatives. By this time, I was friendly with so many families that I was invited to attend a gathering. It was here that I met another Lucio, an ex–chief of police in Brasília.

Lucio

"Come and stay with me for a few days before you go to São Paulo," he said.

I was more than happy to accept, as I was keen to leave the village by now. The work had been done. During the last few days there, I met a wonderful lady in her seventies called Dona Vida from Slovenia who had been sent to Una in Bahia by Sai Baba to set up an ashram there.

"If you don't go to São Paulo, come and visit me," she said. She gave me her address in Bahia on a scrap of paper. I dismissed the idea since it was in the north of Brazil, a long way from Brasília. The time came to go to Brasília with Lucio, the ex-chief of police. By Brazilian standards, his house was well set up. By our standards, we would be appalled. There were thousands of mosquitoes in my room and, everywhere there were flies. So many I smeared myself with repellent and hoped for the best.

He took me around orphanages, old people's homes, and a wonderful temple as well as some most amazing villages, one called Planaltina, to do with healing and space beings.

Planaltina, Goias, Brazil

My full account of the experiences there will have to go into a separate book since it will take a book to enter them all. I may write one specifically about Brazil before I die. Sadly I feel that this too has changed a great deal since I was there.

It turned out that I could not go to the centre in São Paolo after all because of a mix-up, and the lady I was to stay with was in hospital. I discovered this just one day before my flight there. I now feel this was a set-up by my spirit friends. Since I still had two weeks before my return flight and the thought of either returning to the village or staying longer with the chief of police was not an attractive option, the only thing to do was to go to visit the lady Vida in Bahia. Tickets were bought, and phone calls were made. There was so little time that I had no way of knowing if Dona Vida was aware of my coming. After changing planes in Belo Horizonte, I was on my way to a tiny airport called Ilhéus. I sat on the plane and prayed that there would be someone to meet me. I did not know how far I had to go or how to get to the address I had been given.

As I walked out to the carousel on arrival, a young man approached me and said, "Are you Shirley?" I silently thanked my spirit friends and asked him how he knew.

"Lucio phoned me from Brasília and told me to meet the lady in white," he said. He was told to drive me to my destination. I was so grateful, especially when I discovered the address was eighty kilometers away and down what was no more than a track off a main road with just a small wooden sign to direct me to the place. I would never have found it for myself. Once more, it had all been arranged. It was dark when we arrived at the fazenda, and Dona Vida was not at home. After some difficulty and a visit to a nearby village to get someone who worked there to let me in, I was taken back to the fazenda. I was allowed in and shown to a room where I was to sleep until Dona Vida arrived next morning.

Again I was alone in the middle of a plantation, in the dark with only guard dogs to keep me company. I dread to think how I would have fared if spirit had not arranged someone to meet me.

Vida had had no idea of my visit since phone lines were frequently unreliable in that part of Brazil and she had not received the message. (It was years before mobile phones came into being) I was to visit more than once and work there in the two wonderful pyramids. It is an extraordinary place that turned out to be a Sai Baba center, so there he was again in the most unexpected places.

In 2008 I took to the Fazenda Vida a small group from UK who said it was heaven. Another group of 27 people from Slovenia had been invited to meet us all and work together. That is how following one tiny little thread, an address on a scrap of paper, can lead to so much more.

The friendship between Roy and me became strained. I was away too often and, from his perspective, was following a path he could not relate to. He could see that our paths were to go in different directions. We parted good friends and went our separate ways. I shall always be grateful to him for his early teaching. I am sure he is still doing his good work on the other side of the veil.

Chapter 12

Readings

When you feel another's pain try to relieve it.
When you feel another's despair, try to give hope.
When you see the anguish on another's face, try to comfort.
When you feel another's pain, try to relieve it.
When there is confusion, bring clarity.

We could go on. You do not have to look very far to see how you can be of help in your world. Many of you say: I want to be this or that. I want to be a healer, I want to be a teacher, I want to be clairvoyant etc. We say, look around you. There is much that you can do, to alleviate the sufferings of the mind, body and spirit of those who do not know how to help themselves. When you can do this you will find that your spiritual progress has advanced as a result and you are closer to the ideal than you ever thought possible. When you couple your service to development of your psychic senses then may you say, 'I am a Medium for good'. God bless you.
The Little Owl Cards from The White Brotherhood,

Giving readings became a frequent occurrence. I was doing what Josefina said I should. Word was passed around and people began to come.

Anne was one who came. Almost before I had time to ask for help from my guides, a forceful character jumped into my mind.

"Anne, I have a very pushy man here," I told her. "I've had to tell him to wait for me to say my prayer. He says he's having a good time chatting up the ladies," I laughed, seeing him, and gave her a description.

Anne was not surprised. "That's my dad all right. He was just like that when he was alive," she said. "I often feel him around."

Information flowed, providing answers to her unspoken questions.

"Tell her that I really did love her mum, but I enjoyed the fuss other ladies made of me. I got carried away at times. Vanity, I suppose," he said.

"He was a bit of a character," said Anne fondly.

Another reading left me feeling saddened. A lady called Mary brought her mother, who did not want to come alone for a reading. Sydney, an unhappy man in spirit came through, saying, "Why can't she understand? We could have been happy if she had allowed me my one mistake. I thought I was in love with someone else," he explained. "But it was my wife I wanted all along."

Sydney went on to give descriptions of past scenes from their happy times together when Mary was a baby. One scene after another was shown, all depicting their happiness before his slip-up.

"Please forgive me, please remember our good times, not the bad." he pleaded.

His wife wept, but at the end of the reading, she was adamant. She would never forgive him for the hurt he had caused her.

There was no more I could do. She went away as bitter as when she arrived. I felt great pity for them both.

Another lady called Susan looked at me blankly as I passed the information I received. Whatever I said, her expression did not change. This worried me. Was I getting it all wrong? Eventually I came to the end. "Did it answer your questions, my dear?" I asked.

"Oh yes, thank you. You told me all I needed to know," she said, expressionless as before.

Relieved, I was about to show her out when a name popped in. I asked her, "Who's Peter? He is tall but stoops. He says he used to ride a motorbike round and round you to tease you when you were a teenager."

She came alive. "Oh, great! Yes, he was my older brother."

"And who's Ted? He loves gardening. Says he is still working in the garden. He wore old jackets full of bits of string."

"That's my dad," she said, smiling softly.

There followed a string of names with messages and descriptions of each of them.

Why did they leave it to the last minute? I still do not know. Names do not always come; in some readings they never do. Giving names is not my strong point. I was pleased that the information given was accurate.

A common request during a reading is to find out if they will ever meet the man or woman of their dreams, marry, and have a family. I try to assist. On asking my helpers, I will sometimes be given a full description of the partner for them. I am careful not to give dates or names as this might influence choices too much. It is still the responsibility of the client who they join up with or not.

However, I frequently get phone calls saying that they have met the person described, right down to family members, job, and leisure interests.

"It is as if you had a ticker tape in front of you," said one client.

I cannot explain how it happens, but it does. So why can't I do it for myself? It is very important to know that I am not always right. I tell people that, and that whatever they decide to do after a reading has to be their responsibility. I never ever tell them what they should do. They alone must make their decisions. It is perfectly possible that I have it wrong or have interpreted incorrectly. Mind communication is a tricky thing for someone like me, who was not born with psychic abilities fully awakened from the beginning. Responsibility for actions taken because of a reading must lie with the client. For this reason, I do not give readings to anyone who is too young and impressionable.

People get what they need. No two readings are alike. It is a great joy when someone comes striving to be more aware of spiritual matters and wanting to know how they can help others. On these occasions, it is often that a guide will come through and say how they will work with them. A description of the guide is so very helpful since it makes it easier for them to come through when the client meditates.

There are times when I am reluctant to give a reading. I was in Washington DC giving one reading after another, with a full schedule at the Arlington Metaphysical Chapel on Wilson Boulevard that had organized two weeks of appointments. It was hard work but worthwhile!

A very important-looking man sat opposite me. I was impressed, until he asked me to find out certain things. He had not come for the usual reasons. This was political. He told me he worked in a top government position and wanted to know if he should blow the whistle on a situation he had uncovered or keep quiet. If he spoke up, he would lose his position; if he kept quiet, his conscience would eat at him. What should he do?

I was not happy with this situation. I am not a political animal and prefer to keep out of these matters. In much the same way, I do not encourage questions on whether anyone is going to win the lottery. I knew how one could be sued in America for all kinds of things. But this man was adamant; he wanted answers and was used to getting them.

I prayed hard for help and linked in. My guides were wonderful. A picture came into my mind. I told him, "I can see many doors on a second-floor hallway. You have to go into the red one with a red carpet. That is the route you have to take."

I was relieved that they had left it so vague and that I could not know what the picture meant. He continued the sitting with many other questions relating to business ventures, to which they gave me pictures depicting the answers. Perfect. Nobody could sue me for these things, as I was not given anything defamatory which I would have to say on tape. With relief I showed him out. I still to this day get a request for a reading from the same man.

Next day, I had a phone call. It was the politician. My heart sank. What now?

"You were right," he said. "There were many doors and there was a red one. I went through it and it was just as you said. Everything is sorted out, also the business deals you told me about."

I was amazed. I had not expected the pictures given to be literal and had thought they were symbolic only.

My spirit friends proved to be even cleverer than I thought, however. As a result of that sitting, the politician referred another man to me for a reading. I was fully booked at the chapel, so I arranged for him to come to the house where I was staying. I do not like to turn anyone away but prayed he would not be after the same kind of information. He wasn't.

He was impressive. A coal black face on a man in a smart business suit sat opposite me waiting for whatever came. He had wonderful blue eyes. Immediately, a beautiful spirit came, a guide of brilliance and love. I was overwhelmed with wonder at the greatness of this being.

"You will work for the benefit of the world," my visitor was told. "You will open a school for disadvantaged and difficult teenagers." The reading continued in the same vein, giving details of what the project was to be and how it was to begin. My visitor took it all calmly and with great dignity. He has since taken up the challenge. The Booker T. Washington Public Charter School for Technical Arts is flourishing and has even had a visit from the Dalai Lama. I believe the first client was sent simply so that the second one could make the connection with me. It has been a privilege to meet many wonderful people in this work. I am constantly delighted at the beauty of their souls.

Another surprising one was when a young girl came to me when I was still in Washington DC. At first sight, she seemed a most unlikely person to want a reading. She had driven two hours from out of town and was not sure herself why she had come. The surprise began when I saw a most beautiful glowing spirit appear. He introduced himself as the child she was to have in the future. He said he was taking the opportunity while he had it to let her know that he was going to be a very strong personality and if she spoiled him she would ruin his chances of being what he wanted to be. He was coming to earth with a mission, he said. If she did not discipline him, he would be more of a tyrant than of help to the world. He would not know what or who he was until he was seven years of age.

Another sign of special children came when I gave a reading to Julie. I saw she had a child, and spirit told me that her young daughter had a different DNA from the usual. They said she had a special purpose on this planet and to watch for the signs. Julie was ecstatic for she had already had a DNA test done on her daughter and the doctor told her that he had never seen DNA of that form before. It was confirmation. Unfortunately, as I learned later, Julie did spoil the child and, as a result, put back her progress for some time. It eventually righted itself, and I understand the girl is now on track and is a beautiful person and doing well.

It was not only people who came through during a reading. There was one time when the face of a horse appeared right in front of mine. To say it startled me is an understatement. It looked at me with almost human eyes. I told the client who was ecstatic. This was why she had come. Her favourite horse had died, and she always said it looked at her with human eyes. How wonderful that he managed to come through.

So often cats, dogs and other animals present themselves during a reading proving the love bond never dies, or our connection to them.

Another sad visit comes to mind. I was asked by a daughter to give healing to her mother who said she was ill because she missed so much her husband who had died. Would I get in touch with him of the other side? I quickly realised that this lady liked to control people. I explained that as I belonged to the NFSH the rules were that we did not give messages along with the healing. (nowadays I get and give messages if they come relating to the illness, at the same time as healing). I told her I would try when I got home.

This I did, but I would not pass on what he said, but it opened my eyes. He told me:

"I want nothing to do with her. Why does she think I left life so early? It was the only way I could get away from her."

I was to come across this situation more than once. Two people I knew who were in relationships they were not able or courageous enough to get out of silently prayed again and again for release and for a way where they could escape their current way of life. Like the lady who prayed to be waited on and who became paralysed, the subconscious listened and provided what was constantly asked for.

One endured illness over a long period of time until she died. The other had cancer and also died. Both suffered. ***The subconscious listens and acts accordingly.***

Be careful what you ask for and how often. Make sure it is really what you want.

Chapter 13

Conference on the Planet

> We of this evolutionary planet seek out the energy givers, those who can supply the needs of others without hesitation or self-doubting. Here and now we are speaking to you directly if *you* feel yourself to be such a one.
>
> We seek selfless dedication to the task of raising mankind above its previous level of existence. When this has been successfully accomplished, man will have escaped the endless cycle of war, hate, greed, and all those things which degrade the soul.
>
> To be elevated is to experience joy, love, and such harmony in the soul as to be beyond expression in mere words. The value of this opportunity to raise your own soul is immeasurable.
>
> Count on us for full support. God bless you.
>
> *White Brotherhood*

It was deep winter. I sat daydreaming, looking out over my garden at the birds pecking at the food I put out each day. It was bitterly cold; the ground was iron hard. I thanked goodness I was indoors and did not have to go out. It was a good time to meditate.

I was soon "in." Something tickled my cheek. Thinking it

was a stray hair, I brushed it away. It came again. It was then I realized someone was behind me. I turned to see the familiar soft-glowing figure that grew clearer as I looked.

"Andreas!" I cried with pleasure, "I'm so glad you are here. I must tell you. I've met Raman," I said, babbling like an excited child.

Andreas listened quietly and patiently until I dried up. "It is time I gave you some explanation," he said. "Before you go any further, you need to know who we are and who I am."

"You are of the White Brotherhood, aren't you?" I said quickly, my heart thumping uncomfortably. What was coming next? I prayed he would not disappoint me.

"Yes, yes. But you need to know who they are and how they work. I shall explain in stages. It will take quite a time and not a little understanding. It might be difficult to accept."

What could he mean? Hadn't I already accepted him and all that had happened so far? How much more difficult could it be? What was he going to tell me?

"With your permission, I shall take you to meet some people. Is this all right with you?"

"I trust you," I told him, excited now.

"Good. Look at the far wall," he commanded, pointing. I turned and looked. The wall before me began to quiver in an alarming way. Then it disappeared. In its place was a wide flight of steps leading up to a building.

"Go up the steps," Andreas said firmly. He was in charge. There was authority in his voice. "Remember, you are an observer." Andreas stayed close to me. I watched him show his hand to a very tall imposing man standing to the left of a large sliding panel. A button was pressed, and the panel slid open to allow us to enter.

"Where are we?" I asked in a hushed voice.

"It is a conference hall. We are going to look in on a conference concerning your planet. Later if you are up to it, I will take you to talk to several of the members. We will see how it goes first. Once we are inside, please do not speak unless you are addressed. We have a little time yet before we go in."

I looked around, noting how light and airy it was, like day. Being ever practical, I wondered who kept the floor so clean and shiny. Entirely covering one section of a wall was a display screen, rather like a cinema screen.

Andreas saw me looking. "It will present a scene suitable for showing current events," he explained. "See!" He waved his hand at it. A picture appeared.

"It is like switching on the television using remote control," I said.

"Quite so!"

The screen showed a row of men all dressed differently. They were exchanging hats with one another so that they could try them all. Exchanging hats!

"Oh, I see! Exchanging ideas, I exclaimed, pleased that I had caught on quickly. But Andreas was serious, his blue eyes directed at something only he could see. As if to himself, he said, "When nations understand one another's mentalities, when the leaders of nations understand the thinking processes that exist in other lands, then there may be harmony. Greater understanding of traditions must be studied in order to have harmonious relationships. Misunderstanding is born out of ignorance. Knowledge of nationalistic traditions should be gained to avoid the misunderstanding that exists today. Greater interaction is required."

I looked at him with respect. I had never seen him so serious before, so commanding. He continued, "There must be understanding between peoples. If there is no understanding, there cannot be compassion. If there is no compassion, there cannot be love."

On the screen, I saw a long line of children sitting at the feet of the men. It was if they were ready to step into the men's shoes.

"When their fathers have played their part, the children will take over," Andreas said.

"None of the children is wearing a hat, but they are all talking to each other," I observed.

Andreas smiled fondly. "There is already harmony with the children."

"I am no nearer to knowing who the White Brotherhood is," I reminded him.

"Be patient! I need to see how ready you are for the next piece. Please trust me. If I feed you with too much too soon you would suffer physically. Think what would happen if a baby was fed on rich food before it had been weaned. It would be sick and forcibly eject what had been given, or there would be a blockage. What a waste that would be. You understand my meaning?

"You have interpreted the picture given you correctly. Well done! Before we go in, let us talk about the communication rather than the Communicators.

"Communication is for those who are willing to listen or see. It is also for the listener to interpret according to his own beliefs. Identical words or pictures may be interpreted in different ways, according to the heart and mind of the one receiving. It is important that we present knowledge or an idea in such a way as to keep it open to interpretation. We attempt to put forward ideas to be digested, debated and argued over; the more controversial the better. This in itself creates far more interest, more discussion and awakening of minds than anything that is stated too dogmatically.

Sometimes the information given is interpreted in a completely opposite way to the intention. This will happen when the mind of the receiver does not wish to receive what is presented. He will manipulate and remould the idea to his own desire. Think how the Bible and other holy books are understood in so many diverse ways."

Many more people were milling around us and distracted me. It was becoming crowded. Andreas guided me over to a quiet seat. He is no wimp, I decided proudly. I noted that most of the arrivals were in pairs. Andreas touched my arm to bring my attention back.

"There are many occasions when we will use mind pictures. It is a well-known fact that the eye sees only what it wishes to see and is able to completely ignore what it does not recognize or wish to perceive. This may help you to understand why there are so many who receive only part of what we wish to impart. There are many who receive identical information but who interpret it differently to another. We are not allowed to impose or obligate any of you to have that which you are not ready to accept."

I remembered how various clients interpreted differently what they were given in their readings.

He looked at me closely. I sensed he was uncertain whether to continue or not. The crush around us continued to distract my attention. I was excited to see so many strange costumes and colors.

"Shirley, what we have asked you to do is directly connected to how you present the information we give to you. If what we say comes through an incarnated human being, it will be more readily available for debate or acceptance, providing you can present it in a suitable way. It is quite a responsibility and most important. We do not ask this of you lightly. It will require dedication and courage."

Daunted, I doubted if I had the ability. How would I go about it?

Reading my thoughts again, Andreas went on, "You will have assistance. You already have had experience of this. You will be advised what is required. But first, much more preparation is needed. This is why we have taken the unusual step of allowing you to be present at this conference. We wish you to see the importance of our operation."

I had little chance to ask what the operation was, for the crowd began to surge forward. We were on the move. The lighting of the entrance hall in which we were standing changed to an electric blue. It was a signal. A further panel slid open, allowing us to walk through into a large area, like an amphitheater.

I gaped in astonishment at the modern setting before me. A long table was placed across a horseshoe layout with twelve men sitting at the head places. In front of them was an array of switches, consoles, and monitors. At their seats in the hall, many men and women were chatting and fiddling with papers before them. I watched fascinated at the pastel colors playing in constantly moving patterns over the walls of the hall. I wondered if the walls were solid.

Andreas leaned towards me and whispered softly, as we were ushered in and shown to seats lining the walls of light, "There are a great many learned and distinguished men and women here. They have all earned their positions. None of them is without a lifetime or more of dedication."

Other visitors like us were seated along the walls. I saw that they were of many different nationalities. Each had a glowing figure escorting them. I felt honored and humbled at the same time. No one would ever believe this, I told myself ruefully.

"It is a privilege to be here," said Andreas, reading my thoughts.

A man from the top table stood up. There was something familiar about him, but I could not put my finger on it. I felt I knew him. His blue eyes flashed with a strange intensity, but there was the same firm, quiet calmness that Andreas had about him. He wore long, flowing white clothes, which seemed out of place in such a modern setting. All talking ceased as he raised an arm.

His eyes swept the gathering, missing nothing. "This is a big event, a serious event," he began. "We have gathered to discuss the future program for allocating guidance and direction for the planet Earth. You present here are to be given positions of guidance to those who are willing to act as groups and as individuals under your direction. All of you have a large part to play. Each and every one is as important as the other. There is a need for direction and enlightenment as never before. You will direct wisely and with authority that has been earned through many lifetimes of experience and self-learning. You will be aided and directed by a head organization.

"You must not consider that you are in a hierarchy, one more important than another. You will be given areas which are not geographical, but which are areas of thought. You will direct your attentions to minds that are open, and to those who have greatest need for conversion of thought. It is an important role that you are playing.

"The planet Earth is in difficulties. We have a responsibility to do something to assist it before it loses all life-forms. However, we do not have the right to exert our will over any individual, even if that individual is bent on destruction. We can merely present the possibilities so that mankind may make decisions necessary to avert disaster, or at least lessen the impact of its actions. Moreover, we also have a responsibility to all the planetary systems, not only to that of the local universe."

I watched as this glorious figure turned around to face the wall behind him. He waved a hand at the wall in the way that Andreas had outside this arena; the entire wall became a huge screen. I was caught up in the stillness of the audience, the words ringing in my ears. All other things seemed so unimportant by comparison.

I stared at an enormous figure projected onto the wall. I could not see his face because it was lit so brightly. He was demonstrating his position by standing on a globe with his arms outstretched, fingers pointing. As he pointed, he touched the other planets and stars as they passed by. The globe he was standing on revolved beneath his feet. He was controlling the movements of the universe. I knew he could change planetary movements at will.

A deep powerful voice echoed throughout the great hall and set my spine tingling, sending a thrill throughout my whole body. "I will not exercise by whim, but I *may* exercise my will if it is required. I may adjust the position of any given planet according to my best judgment. I am to make it clear to man in a language he can understand that man is not controller of the Earth or of the universe. He is not in command. There is a higher authority. This same authority has instructed me to act in kindness and love for furthering the creation to its best advantage, not for destruction. I am also given the responsibility of looking for the greatest benefit to the whole of creation, not only for one portion of it, such as the planet Earth."

The booming voice vibrated through the entire assembly. From where I sat, I could see that all eyes were on the screen, transfixed.

"The souls of man do not reside on the planet Earth alone. They do not reside on Earth's astral plane or in third dimension alone. They reside on many other levels and on many other planets besides. Therefore, we must look to the greater whole. At times, some adjustment is necessary for the smoother running of the entire system. I have the authority and the responsibility to ensure this. I will do it with love, compassion, and understanding, but I will also do it with a firmness that will not be shaken. It is for each individual here to understand the overall system and to understand his or her role in it. We are showing you this representation not for amusement, but so that you may take heart and know that there is to be a continuation of mankind."

The picture faded. The hall was hushed. Everybody present needed time to absorb the importance of that stirring message. The atmosphere was charged. I bubbled with many questions. Who or what did this figure represent? There were so many things I did not understand. I remembered in time I was not to speak and kept silent.

Another bearded speaker from the top table stood up. He too seemed familiar. I was certain I had seen him before but could not say where. He was dressed in a similar way to the first speaker but in pale blue, matching his eyes. Golden, wavy hair fell over his shoulders. Strong and virile, he too spoke with firmness and directness to the attentive audience.

"For the benefit of our visitors, I wish to clarify something."

I wondered if he had read my thoughts. I listened intently, aware of Andreas by my side. "We twelve have been given a collective name. We prefer not to be individualized for we work as one. We interact with other teams to work in harmony and unity for the benefit of all mankind. I repeat that we prefer that you think of us as one team spirit."

Was this the White Brotherhood, I wondered?

"You might regard us as heads of a vast organization. We are very orderly and not at all random. We have our project plans and achievement levels. Those of you in business will understand that one must be forever striving. We strive not for monetary gain but to redeem the planet and the peoples upon it.

"We strive, but the peoples upon the planet have it in their own hands to redeem their souls. They have free will over their conduct but do not have command over the Earth. *The planet that they are on is not to be their only dwelling place.* Our project is twofold. The planet itself must be protected; for your planet is an important place for the growth of souls. It is not merely just another planet for there are many, but it is a special area for growth. It has a variety of different conditions (environments) that may be enjoyed or otherwise. It has enormous potential for learning. It is constantly changing, a kaleidoscope of wonder.

"We do not wish to see the life go out on Earth, or for it to become a dead and dull sphere. We strive to keep it alive and will do what is necessary. Know too that the souls of man will continue to incarnate until a greater stage of evolution is reached. It is far better for them to incarnate on a pleasant and beauteous world than on one that would not be so enjoyable."

Smiling, he continued to address us all, "You are wondering why you are here." It was a statement, not a question. "You will be given further information, showing you your tasks and the reasons for them. You will be able to ask questions of the helpers allocated to you. There will be opportunities for direct contact in times of need with those in control. This contact depends upon your own level of physical, mental, and spiritual preparation. You are to be used as communicators on a physical level to your fellow man. You are to pass the information given to you to those in your world who do not have the ability to receive directly from us.

"I now ask that your guardians escort you from this assembly. Sufficient has been shown you for the moment." He smiled kindly at us all lined up along the walls.

I was disappointed at having to leave but was led firmly out along with the others. The panel closed behind us as we left.

"Come," said Andreas holding me by the elbow. He led me

through yet another panel that silently slid open at a pass of his hand. This place is all panels, I thought to myself. Feeling rather self-conscious, I passed my hand over the walls to see if I could operate something. Nothing happened. Andreas grinned as he saw me do this.

We entered a circular room, empty except for two modern swivel chairs in the center. All around the walls was a continuous screen. This is fantastic, I thought, marveling at the technology. I pretended to brush a hair from my face, still hoping to activate some hidden mechanism with my hand.

"You do not have the vibration needed to operate the Looking Glass," Andreas said, smiling when he realized what I was trying to do. He indicated the chairs. "Sit down, if you will."

I was bursting with questions. "How is it that every one of the visitors understood what was being said? They must all have different national languages. They cannot all speak English, surely?"

"Such a small point," said Andreas with a sigh. "In an international assembly on your Earth, each one attending has earphones through which an interpreter relays the talk. Here the message is conveyed by thought to all minds present. Thought does not have a language but is conveyed by vibration, which reaches the minds and is translated into the language of the one on the receiving end. To you it appears that the speaker is using your own language, for that is what you are hearing. This process also works in reverse. Your own thoughts are received and understood without you ever speaking a word. Would you by now agree that I know what you are thinking?" He watched me carefully.

I had to agree that this was so. Hadn't he proved it over and over again? It also explained why Raman the Rajah, Wang Lu, and Abdul all came over to me in English despite it not being their national language. Satisfied with my understanding,

Andreas sat beside me, faced the screen, and waved. I wondered what I would be shown next.

The screen cleared to show a solidly built elderly figure. His hat was dome shaped. It looked as if his head was shaped that way. When he began to speak, all my attention was on his face. The extra-large clear green eyes held me fast. I could not look elsewhere, even if I had wanted to.

"We will begin with an explanation of what is to come. There are to be changes upon the planet, which to some will appear to be catastrophic, yet to others who are prepared they will be welcome, even a necessity. There have always been changes during the existence of your planet, but life has never been totally permanently destroyed, merely adapted and changed. Is this not so?"

I did not know if I was expected to reply to a screen display. So I stayed quiet and waited.

"We wish mankind to continue. We wish to alleviate distress and calm panic. We wish, in short, to be fathers to the souls who are incarnated upon the planet to have experiences there. If the souls of mankind suffer too great a trauma, their onward progression may be adversely affected. We ask for volunteers to come forward for service on the physical plane, to encourage their fellow men to reach a greater serenity and a greater knowing, to know that whatever happens on their physical world, their souls will continue and incarnate again."

It seemed to me that the old man trembled with passion as he spoke. I wished I could put out a hand to soothe him.

"Think of Earth as a sick patient. The patient cannot remain in the state it is in now. It has had ills inflicted upon it. It is receiving surgery with parts being cut away from it. There are parasites and irritations that it cannot rid itself of. It is being slowly poisoned. We feel for this poor planet, and we wish to restore it to its former strength and beauty. We will not allow it to die. We have authority to make changes that will restore it to full strength so that mankind and other species may flourish yet again. Surely this is a glorious thing? Far better than allowing the patient to die, which is what may happen if mankind has its way."

Speaking with great feeling, the old man continued, "Naturally, souls may continue to incarnate on any world. The planet Earth is not necessary for this, but it is a beauteous thing with many varieties upon it. It is a gem that is much loved. We wish to restore this gem to its full brilliance so that souls may visit and grow amidst the beauty. I beg you all to look after it." He raised his arms in an imploring gesture.

I reached for Andreas and clutched his hand. I held tight to his fingers as the old man went on.

"We repeat: We ask for volunteers, for pioneers who are not afraid to open their mouths and say what is in their hearts. It matters not if you are ridiculed, for you will go to the end of your days with the knowledge that you did what you could. You *cannot* be given this knowledge and hold it within yourself. You would not want to ask yourself in other times and other places why you knew and did nothing, for you would regret this. Do not fear the ridicule of others, for that is a minor thing."

The screen was suddenly switched off, much to my relief.

"Whew! That was a bit strong," I said. My head was beginning to reel. I felt hot. I knew I could not take much more.

Andreas, realizing my condition, got up from his chair. "We will go," he said as he put his arm gently round my waist. The next thing I knew, I was propped up against cushions in my favorite chair. Had I fainted? It was all like a dream. Had it really happened?

Chapter 14

Space Stations

Eyes that you do not see are upon you. Every move is noticed. Where your actions are to assist someone else, angels' eyes light up with joy and delight. They know that all is not lost upon the planet earth and the heart is lightened.

The Little Owl Cards

Later that day, I meditated on the question as to where all this was leading me. I noticed Raman sitting on a stool by the window, looking resplendent as usual in his white leggings and coat. I stifled a smile at the incongruity of the picture. Did he really have to dress like that, I wondered?

"Hello!" I said, inclining my head and pretending to bow. How was one to address a full-blown rajah?

As upright and imposing as ever, Raman returned my greeting. "It is good to be with you again," he said formally. "I understand that you have done a course in public speaking."

News gets around fast, I thought. "Yes." I said, wary now.

"One does not learn to speak in public unless one intends to do so, does one?" He looked at a nearby patterned mug and studied it carefully. Trying to be casual, he said, "You will need to write down all we have told you, especially if you are going to speak out."

I opened my mouth to say something and thought better

of it. Seeing this, Raman grunted reprovingly. "It is time you were shown a new perspective," he said, as one used to being in command. He stood up and touched my arm. He who should be obeyed, I thought, amused.

Changing tactics like one maneuvering, he said with a quiet gentleness, "Close your eyes and put your hands together on your lap." He placed warm hands round my head. The pressure mounted until it reached bursting point. How much more could I take?

"Be patient," he whispered.

Moments passed. "All right, you can open your eyes now."

The pressure disappeared, and so had the room. I could see a sky filled with what looked to me like platelets, drifting horizontally. I watched, fascinated, as they floated together until they interlinked with one another, forming a complete platform. It reminded me of pieces of a jigsaw puzzle fitting neatly together. I was baffled. It did not make any sense to me. I got to my feet and paced up and down as I tried to see it from another angle.

"It is a life-support system," he explained, "one that can be dismantled and maneuvered. Also, it can have parts added to it or replaced. It is very adjustable, is it not?" His eyes sparkled with pride. "It is not as simple as it appears. Within the main body, there are many complex systems for administration purposes. There are circuits which are self-motivating, self–replenishing, and self-repairing independently, or dependent on the mind and will of those who manage these systems."

I looked up, fascinated at the shapes drifting silently above me. "What is it all for?" I asked, awestruck. They were so huge.

"As I have said, it is a support system."

"Support for what?" I persisted.

Raman cleared his throat. He told me to sit down again as it was going to take some time to explain. I perched myself rather uncomfortably on a low wall that had conveniently appeared. Raman began to pace up and down before me.

"There are numerous space stations called life-support systems surrounding your planet and your universe. You might call them mother ships. There are many in existence, used for intermingling and traveling, not only from one zone to another in a manner related to new physics, but also through dimensions of time. Each system is manufactured for a specific purpose. We convert one system to another frequently, according to changing needs. For example, should a group of our specialists need to visit a certain zone, they may do so using one of these platforms. They do not move in a physical sense such as your astronauts do, for it would take too long. They use instead a means of immediate transfer through will/mind power which, combined with certain procedures, enable their intention to be put into action. It takes but a fraction of what you term *time*. We are giving you here, a broad outline only. You understand we cannot give you details. It is also doubtful if you could understand, in any case." He stopped pacing and stood in front of me. He saw I was becoming restless and fidgety. "Had I understood so far?" his expression said.

"Please go on," I said encouraging him.

He looked around for a smooth dry patch of ground, dusted it with a white cloth and sat down cross-legged before starting again. "When the need arises for physical interaction and changing the layers of being, that is, changing dimensions, such as when I visit you, we use a specific platform adapted for this, which has equipment especially installed. You may compare it to a pressure chamber such as your deep-sea diver's use. It is not quite the same but may help you understand. The procedure is highly technical. The technology has been achieved by beings whose mind power and thought processes have been fully utilized.

"On certain designated platforms, we are able to bring ourselves into a vibration where we can be recognized by mortal beings. There have been many times when this has been necessary. We make use of your five physical and inner senses for recognition on these occasions."

Since that time I learnt that some of our cosmic friends can indeed move beyond densities and are called Extra-dimensionals. In other words they are beyond dimensions and do not need any form unless they choose. I have much to learn on this.

I studied my unusual friend with added interest. I had not realized he knew so much and understood it, which was more than I did.

Raman shot a keen look at me and continued, "It is easier for us to contact your world by using your inner senses, not those at a conscious level. For the most part, this is the method we have used with you personally. Meditation is a wonderful means of achieving the physical and mental state required, is it not?"

I thought to myself, "There's not much chance of me meditating right now, this wall is much too hard," and then I wondered at that since I was operating in the nonphysical during this interaction.

"It is your mind," Raman said, interrupting my thought. "You still haven't broken away from thinking in physical terms, and so your experience will feel physical. When you learn to think in higher energy forms, then you will not experience physical reality in the mind."

I had forgotten completely that I was already in meditation and had entered another world.

He went on, "There are other densities, other realms, each having their own rate of vibration and their own pressure rate. These are at times interchangeable with your own planetary bands, when they can react and interact with each other. Your planet is ruled by time. Your minds would consider it unfeasible for a rapid interchange over vast areas of time and space. Yet this is possible using what you might call star gates or portals.

"Access to these systems will be available when more of you become proficient at communicating with the inner senses, more information will be given directly to you. You will be able to gain entry to it for yourselves in much the same way as when one learns a computer system, the information within becomes available. Meditation was the key to open your door to us. We were waiting for you to do that. You took such a long time to realize we were around that we almost gave up." He rubbed his thick beard thoughtfully. After a while, he stood up and renewed his pacing.

I reflected it was a lucky day when I attended the class where I experienced meditation for the first time and realized it was not a bizarre thing to do after all.

"Your own body is gradually being adjusted to the changes. Soon you will have no barrier or pressure to overcome. Your mind will do it all. Do not be concerned if you feel discomfort from time to time as we take you through the process."

I was not concerned about discomfort anymore. I forgot the hard wall. I wanted to know more about the life-support systems. Were these the UFO's that people had been seeing for so long? What was floating above us sounded and felt more like a mother ship. I had no idea that later I would visit just such a station, where much more would be explained to me. *See Calling Earth*

I stood up and began pacing alongside him. I wondered if anyone could see me, for I had long accepted all this was going on in the mind. I had to ask. "Are you a physical reality or just spirit, or what? Why are all of you presented as human beings from recorded history?"

"They are good questions." He smiled his pleasure and slowed his pace to match mine. "You are clearly paying attention. We represent all worlds, physical and of the spirit. Those of us in spirit are engaged jointly with physically incarnated beings in sending communication," he replied obscurely. He again ran his hand through his thick beard. It was quite a habit with him, I noted.

"First of all, those presented to you so far have had life experiences on the Earth. Some of us, such as Abdul el Faraz, had a life connection with you personally. It is natural for them to present themselves as you knew them, even if you do not remember them. Andreas is your own personal guardian and will remain with you. You called him your angel once."

I blushed furiously. I did not think anyone knew that. I gazed up at the sky to watch the vast life-support system still hanging silently above.

Tactfully Raman did not comment on my red face. "Others having had Earth experiences and working for the benefit of mankind may adopt an appearance from any one of their lifetimes and will generally take on the one that had the most beneficial impact on the world. You will experience more of this later.

"Some of us take on the form that represents to the human mind an aspect of wisdom and learning. It is for this reason that many who have made an appearance are often Native Americans, Chinese, Tibetan, Indian, Egyptian, and Greek, and so on. It is generally accepted that these ancient cultures had a knowledge that has been lost today. If we gave you a John Smith down the street, he would not be taken seriously by you, no matter how wise he might be."

My legs began to ache with all the walking. I would have liked to link my arm with the Rajah's, but I did not dare. That might be going too far. I looked up again at the sky. The "system" had vanished; all I could see were stars.

Raman had not finished yet. "May we also say that the belief system you hold in your mind will convert the thought pattern that is attempting to communicate with you into a recognizable being, in keeping with your belief, hopes, and expectations. This is overridden when the ability to see more fully has been developed.

"Those who restrict themselves to communication with so-called dead relatives or departed loved ones, come under a different category. As for ourselves, we wish to make contact for a wider purpose. I am sure you see what I am saying. This concept can be a little complicated, therefore I will delay a full explanation just now, for I see you are tired."

At last he realizes that I am human, I thought. "What has public speaking got to do with all this?" I asked.

He scratched his chin again in feigned exasperation and sighed. "Do you think that we have gone to so much trouble to explain all this to you just for our amusement? You have a role to play in our plans. We cannot exert our will on you or oblige you to do what you do not want to do. Some trust in us is required. I cannot say more." With another big sigh, he returned me home to reflect. I had a lot to think about. I remembered Andreas had cautioned me earlier.

"You cannot teach spiritual truths to those who do not seek. They will hunger for truth when they have had sufficient life experience," he warned. "Take care not to frighten or make uneasy by disclosing too soon what has been revealed to you. Wait until the way is open."

Dejected, I wondered when that was likely to be. Use your judgment wisely, he had said. I decided I was not much good at judging anything.

Physical Preparation

A week or two passed with no further word from my spirit friends. I noticed that there was a pattern of maintaining a gap in communication between one piece of training and the next. It was as if I had to assimilate what had been given before they would give any more. Realizing this may help others in the same situation. I felt a loss when I could not make a connection and wondered each time if I had done something wrong.

It rained with a persistence that seemed never to end. The trees dripped as if crying and seemed to me that they were bowed down in sorrow. The air was damp and gloomy outside. I turned the central heating up higher and settled down for a quiet evening. I was comfortable and warm, consoled by the absolute peace in the room. I reflected on Raman and the smart neat clothing he always wore. As if in response to my thoughts, he appeared before me, standing very upright and proud with the jewel in his turban glinting brightly. He must have replaced it with another, I thought.

He addressed me formally. “Good evening, my child.”

“Hello,” I replied dismally. “How nice it is to see you.”

Raman looked at me closely, detecting my mood. “Are you ready for another preparation?” he asked. Before I could answer, he added, “This one is physical.”

“What are you going to do? What is it for?” I looked at him anxiously.

“You need to become adjusted to a higher frequency for closer and easier communication,” he explained. “We need to do this in easy stages. There are others we wish you to meet, but you cannot do so without prior preparation.”

“All right,” I said, perking up at last. I wondered why I had to be prepared.

“Stay calm,” instructed Raman.

I felt his hands on my shoulders. My chest began to hurt; I struggled to breathe. My head began to fill to the point of bursting. "What's happening to me?" I cried silently. My lungs turned icy cold, enveloping me. The cold reached down into my stomach. Now I knew what it was like to be deep-frozen. My arms became numb as if drained. I nearly cried out with the ache in my throat. I lost all sensation, then blanked out.

Soon I was back with Raman, still frozen with cold.

"Phew!" I said, shivering violently. "Was all that necessary?"

"Quite essential." he replied. "You did well to stay with it, for we have achieved what we set out to do. You can now reach much higher vibrations to make the connection we need you to have. You could have ended it any time just by thinking that you could not stand anymore," he explained.

Now he tells me, I thought.

"I will leave you to recover. We have done well and will make real progress now."

I went straight to bed, put the electric blanket on and wrapped the duvet tightly round me. I slept soundly.

I woke to the birds singing long before it was time to get up. I felt alive once more, and vibrant. I rose and drew back the curtains to see a steady wall of rain still falling. I did not know what Raman had done, but whatever it was, I felt great. I was full of energy all day and got through a lot of household tasks I had been putting off. That evening after a hot cup of tea, I settled down in my usual chair and stayed quiet, not expecting too much. I should have known it was always when I least expected it that the most amazing things happened.

I have come to recognise when I go into a much higher state, or should I say deeper level?

Chapter 15

Discernment and Caution

There is at times a need to take risks. If you always take the safe route, then your life's journey would become uneventful. Do not be afraid to step into the unknown. If you have already committed yourself to some venture which you now consider to be foolhardy, take heart for this is where your trial of strength and purpose will be. Remember, nothing can hurt you except yourself. *White Brotherhood*

I felt a soft touch on my shoulder. "Wake up, my dear," a voice said.

I opened my eyes to find myself standing before a number of men sitting behind a long table. They looked at me with such kindness that I wanted to cry. Controlling my emotions, I smiled, uncertain of myself.

"Come forward," they beckoned me over. "We have called you to us to explain that the path you have accepted is bound up with our program for your planet and the peoples on it. You and others like you are now considered to be part of our organization. Some might say that what we do is interfering with the will of man. We stress that this we are not doing, for man still retains the right of free choice as an individual. We put ideas and suggestions before them, and it is up to them to accept, act or ignore.

"It is necessary for you to know that not all in our world think as we do. We wish to caution you. We understand that you are quickly perfecting the ability to make your own connections with those of nonphysical form and those beyond your planetary system. Therefore it is vital you are aware that not all created souls have followed the divine path which was set before them. There have been deviations from the original concept, which have continued to grow in strength since the first beginnings towards evolution. There are confused and misguided souls who, in their journeys, have acquired a great strength of negative energy, which may be as powerful as our own."

The others nodded in agreement, muttering among themselves.

"You are aware that energy is neutral and can be used in both negative and positive ways. It is wise to take note of this fact. We urge you to use your energies according to your own conscience and beliefs and not that of others, who may be misguided or influenced by powerful negative forces. Do not make the mistake of thinking that because your communication comes from a non-physical source that it is always beneficial. You will need to use your own judgment more than ever.

"Each soul, physical or otherwise, must make its own decisions and follow its own course. Please note that we have advised you that we are not alone in the influence field."

The gentle blue-eyed speaker leaned forward across the table. His strong serene face helped to calm the fluttering inside me.

"We come to the next point. We spoke earlier of those outside your universe. There are many worlds besides your own. These too have physical form and contact with their spirit world. Many of these worlds are greatly concerned about the state of your planet, knowing that the entire creation must have complete harmony. Where there is disharmony, whether it is on a planetary level or on a minute level, such as an infection on your finger, the well-being and smooth running of the greater whole is affected."

I noticed for the first time a vast map of heavenly bodies on the wall behind them. I wondered how they kept track of them all if they were responsible for their safekeeping. It made my own little problems pale into insignificance.

He waited patiently for me to bring my attention back to him. "Shall we take the comparison of infection? Even a minute infection on a part of a physical being is acutely felt by the total sum of that body. Where the infection spreads, the mind and thoughts are also disturbed. The vibrations that the body gives off are not then harmonious to those around it. It produces an irritation which affects others not of the same physical body.

"So it is with disharmony, disease, and discord on your planet. This discord is felt by other parts of your universe. Thoughts and feelings have an energy wavelength that has no limit to its direction and range. Uncomfortable waves of energy are received by all within the path of these vibration rays. No world escapes. The greater whole is affected in the same way that an infection on the finger can upset the entire body if left unattended.

"This is an extremely simplified comparison, but it serves for the moment. What you are given today is preparing you for communication from those other worlds. We do not wish you to be alarmed when it occurs. Do not be disturbed by physical appearance but decide on their good intent or otherwise by using your judgment."

Leaning forward again, he said kindly, "If you are not too tired, we will continue."

My throat was dry. "Please go on," I croaked. I did not want to stop now.

"Our own thoughts directed to you are to be vocalized through you. This serves a purpose. It ensures accurate representation of what we must show and say, to all who may wish to benefit from this. Recounting from memory distorts. We will rest with you now. We urge you to continue to verbalize your experiences as they occur."

I remembered how my life was before entering this new world. I had been afraid to speak up. I had suffered in silence and had paid for it. Did I really want to go back to being that way? I knew I did not.

Chapter 16

Enter Dr. Po

Can I see another's woe
and not be in sorrow too?
Can I see another's grief
and not seek for kind relief?
William Blake

Dr Po

I got up each day at the same early hour, intending to fill every moment. All was peaceful as I sat down one morning to meditate. I had just finished concentrating on healing for those who had requested it, when I became aware of a figure calmly watching me from the side. I remained quite still and waited, hardly daring to breathe. From the corner of my eye, I saw the figure moving closer until it was facing me. I could not pretend it was not there anymore. He was not very tall, but imposing nonetheless. He lowered drooping eyelids over sad eyes and stood silently, allowing me time to study him closely. His expression was doleful and rather somber. High cheekbones over hollow cheeks did nothing to alleviate this impression. A droopy thin moustache and long, narrow beard gave him the appearance of a learned man. If his long, richly brocaded clothing was anything to go by, he was a Tibetan of some distinction. I decided to call him Dr.Po because of his po face. I felt he might not be amused if I told him this. At this thought, his prim mouth went up slightly at the corners in the slightest suggestion of a smile. I had the distinct feeling that he had registered what was going through my mind.

At last he opened his eyes. Eyes like dark buttons glittered under heavy, sagging lids. I knew I was standing before a teacher and should not speak unless invited to do so. He was to be treated with respect.

He began in a light high voice, "Good evening." He allowed himself a toothy grin, tucked his arms inside long sleeves, and bowed slightly. "Would you care to come with me, little one?" he asked. It was strange to be called little one at my age, but I rather enjoyed it. I sensed the love that came with his presence and felt warm towards him. I was going to like this new visitor. I nodded in agreement, ready for anything.

The scene changed instantly, startling me. Once more, I found myself in the same circular screen room I had visited with

Andreas. Furtively, I tried again to wave my hand at the walls, hoping I had acquired some skill since my last visit to impress my new companion. No luck. The walls remained blank except for a single red light in the upper-right corner.

"Mountains may move," said the little Tibetan as he turned to face the wall. "Much which had gone unnoticed will suddenly strike the eye, and you will wonder why it is that you had not seen earlier. When life is turned the other way up, many things fall into light. That which was hidden will be uncovered. So, in the turning, do not be afraid. A shifting of position is a great leveler, in all respects. A leveling is a humbling which does no one any lasting damage but which at the time may cause some discomfort of pride.

"There is to be a reversal. Those who were of lowly status will find themselves in positions of esteem, where respect is given. They will not be tempted by exalted ego. They will understand and will not look down on their fellowman who are now in the positions they once endured."

A shiver ran down my spine. Was this advance warning of some great upheaval? The eminent Tibetan remained facing the wall. There was more to come.

"During your period of stability, gain as much wisdom as you can so you are best able to comprehend in times of change. Those who have gained a greater understanding will be in a favored position. We do not say this in terms of having advantage over others but in terms of being of assistance to those who require it, who are in need, and who do not understand. It will be a position of service and sacrifices, in the knowledge that what you do for others you do for yourself also. So there can only be gain. We are aware that your interpretation upon this will be clear. We thank you for your ears and look to you for your voice."

The red light went out on the screen. Dr. Po bowed slightly

as if to an unseen audience. I was sure he had been filmed. He turned at last to face me.

"So many questions in your mind, little one," he said, squinting at me. His dour face revealed no expression, but I detected an underlying dry sense of humor.

"What you have heard is simply one of our transmissions. Because most of us operate from a dimension other than your own and are of a higher rate of vibration, you must not assume that we are less real. We are as much a reality as you and all things of Earth. You are aware that in communicating with you and others like you, we operate on thought waves and pure energy forms.

"I know you have already visited one of our conference halls where we group together to organize and plan, where we decide how we may best help our fellow souls. This particular centre is concentrating its efforts on the planet Earth and the effect it is having on other cosmic bodies."

I puzzled as to how this ancient Tibetan came into the scheme of things. Why was he still in the dress of past times?

"Time is not of relevance here," he said, picking up my thought. We dress in what we feel to be most comfortable, and often what resonates with you because of our past interaction with each other. Many of us from your history have an interest in your future. Those from the past can come forward to assist you, just as you from your present life have crossed the time barrier. Time does not prevent us from uniting in a common cause. What you do now will affect your future. You yourself have been crossing time again and again since you first began communicating."

Fascinated, I interrupted him. "The quivering walls and mirrors through which I passed, were they to do with crossing time?" I remembered the reference to a Looking Glass. Later I was informed that the Looking Glass was a device used by the military to see into a possible future, and what they saw terrified them.

His dark eyes looked sharply at me. "Not always. Through your preparation, you were able to cross dimensions. Time change occurred if it was relevant, otherwise it did not. We controlled things. Be quite clear about this."

He paused and drew his thin body up. I wondered if he felt fatigued under all that heavy brocaded clothing.

"The human mind is conscious of sequence and duration, of movement from one event to another in time. The human spirit knows of time as a movement towards increasing divinity. It is too simplistic to say that there is no such thing as time. We say only that there need not be a barrier to journeying in time. The soul consciousness can travel, learn, or communicate with any time frame or space.

"If the mind is well directed, it may benefit from taking a time journey, providing always that it returns to the current lifetime to put into action that which it has learnt. The same rule applies to forward travel, into the future. The possible future is given to you for viewing, specifically to enable you to prepare or adapt your thinking. It is not fixed, does not have to happen, and is dependent on your thinking today." Once again I thought of the Looking Glass.

I decided to get a word in. "There is much talk about a plan. Can you tell me anything about it?" I hesitated, unsure just how far to go.

"Sit down, little one." He indicated the two swivel chairs in the center of the room. "Make yourself comfortable, for this may take some time." He smiled to himself, pleased with the pun. "You may not be able to sustain the energy required to complete this viewing, but we will see. We will use the Looking Glass."

I stifled a giggle as he positioned himself stiff and erect alongside. What would the girls in my old office say if they could see me now, sitting next to an old man from another time surrounded by high technology? I could hardly believe it myself as I looked sideways at him out of the corner of my eye.

He waved his thin hand slowly; the screen came alive. A feeling of unreality swept over me. This felt physical. Lightheaded as if in a dream world, I found it difficult to focus. What was happening to me? I squeezed my eyes tight, trying to clear my head. When I opened them again, I found everything had changed.

I stood on open ground. The air was dry, making it difficult to breathe. The place seemed empty until a scrawny little dog tottered over to me. The pathetic little bundle tried to get my attention. He must be a stray, I thought as I bent down to stroke him, almost afraid of hurting him, he was so thin. Poor thing! He was terrible to see. He trotted off on wobbly legs. I followed him through a gap in a walled enclosure.

The scene in front of me appalled me. There were many others like him, not just dogs but people as well. Scrag bags of humanity, all alive but skeletal and obviously starving. They looked up with enormous eyes as I came through the gap, as if I reminded them of a past comfortable existence where there was food and no worries. I could see they had given up hope and existed moment to moment.

I stood there helpless, wondering what I could do. Their eyes told me their minds were still there, complete with memory. All the knowledge they ever had still remained, no matter what had happened. Each head contained a vast store of memories, experiences, knowledge, and wisdom. Even this moment was being stored in their cells and in their soul memory. This really focused for me an important part of existence, the part that endures no matter what happens to the flesh. The consciousness and the soul memory are not eradicated. What could I do to help them?

Dr. Po's high voice startled me. "You can pray for them with compassion. That is the greatest thing you can do at this time. There are great souls here, who have come to move others to compassion so that changes may be made."

With that, I realized that I had returned swiftly to the circular viewing room. Dr. Po was patting my hand with his incredibly long fingers. He peered at me, his face close to mine. A sweet smell from him wafted over me. I thought it probable that he used oils of some kind.

"The dizziness will pass," he assured me. I leaned back in my chair until the woozy sensation subsided. I tried to focus my eyes.

"We spoke earlier of mind power, did we not? Much later, we will experience the next items as observers. It will be less draining for you," he added sympathetically.

"It is time to go back. We will meet again when you have fully recovered."

Chapter 17

Predictions

> Make haste and act before it is too late. Give of your best in all things with hope and trust in a perfect outcome. Now is not the time for sitting and waiting in spite of all you have been told. Complete your unfinished projects, wrap them up and step forth. Now is the time for action. Do not be influenced by contradictory views for you are the one to make things happen, not others. Set your mind on your journey and plan the route. Take whatever path will get you there. Do not sit back and wait.
> Our love goes with you.
> *The Little Owl Cards from White Brotherhood*

By now I was channeling three evenings a week and meditating twice a day. At each of these sessions, there was so much information coming through that it took all my spare time to transcribe it from the tapes. Dr. Po was with me for most of these sessions and was seen and described by those present. He is to this day still seen frequently over me or in the audience when I channel. He is able to visibly leave me and go down and touch others who may need healing or comfort. Those who experience this see him and feel him.

During these times, I saw a great deal of what could happen to the Earth in future years. A great deal of emotion comes through to me when I view these scenes. The method used by spirit communicators was to give me a scene that I either understood immediately or did not. When I did not understand, I asked questions and was often given an explanation. These could be long or short. Some of the events shown have already come to pass and some still to do so unless we change things with our actions and minds.

I was told that predictions are given as warnings rather than events that are inevitable. They may be compared to scare tactics used by the media to stop smoking, drug misuse, or bad driving habits. They are geared to shock the public into taking note and so act in a different way. Our future is dependent on how we act today. It is with this in mind that I present the predictions as given to me. I really do not want to project doom and gloom but given that some of the events are down to man and can be changed if they have the will, I feel it is worth including them for consideration. Nothing is cast in stone, and we can all change things if we try.

All that is presented here is exactly as given by spirit and has not been altered in any way.

The Russian Bear: A Prediction

I see the Russian bear. It has got spears in it. It is fighting off attacks by the people.

It is an enormous bear, but it has been tamed. People are throwing sticks and spears at it. They are angry. It is roaring, it is mighty, and the people are very small, very tiny, but they are hurting it. The sun is low, but it is coming up. It is rising. There are black clouds, but the sun is rising, and the heat of the sun will melt the clouds. The bear will not be slain. It will be tamed, domesticated, and fed by the people. It will be tamed by the spears and stones, by the small people. The black clouds will remain until the heat of the sun is strong. It will take generations, generations under the black clouds. Those in the south will feel the heat of the sun before those in the north. And the west and the east will have a mixture of cloud and clear sky, but it will take a generation.

The great bear will survive, and must be fed. It is large; it requires a lot of feeding. It will grow thin before the time is finished, but it will grow sleek again when the sun is hot. It will sleep when the sun sets, but it will remain well until the sun rises again in the east. The people, though they are small will not be slain by the bear."

NB. This was given before USSR was broken up by the people. I wonder what the sun represents.

Movement of Peoples: August 21, 1991

I am in the Hall of Knowledge in the altered state and describe what follows.

"I see a tall ship, it is packed. It is on a stormy sea at night. It is packed with people from the black countries, dark skins. They are looking to the west. They will come across stormy waters to settle and remain in the lands of their discovery. It is their new world of discovery. They will prosper. They will bring music and color. They will be many. They will grow and cultivate. They will cultivate the fields as in their former lands using the same methods, living the same lives, singing the same songs. They will teach their ways. It is a reversal of the past."

For me it is like a television screen; the pictures start there and become real. It is strange; it is like watching a big video that you enter and become a part of.

Chinese Prediction: August 21, 1991

"The Chinese are highly evolved. They do not need to leave their lands. They will be invited to assist, to advise those outside their lands. They will be esteemed, they will give their counsel when *they* so desire, when *they* wish to do so. They feel self-sufficient and spurn the activities of the outside world. They are a world unto themselves.

"Their numbers will diminish in ways not related to birth control. It will be a blessing, a salvation. Even the people will see it as a salvation. It will be their strength. The intelligence will flourish like a flower. The wisdom will be ever present. The warlike emotions, aggressiveness will not be present, will not be necessary. They have no need (*for aggression*), no reason, nothing to gain and everything to lose. Their wisdom will be admired and respected and sought after. They will be honored as peers."

America—Prediction: August 21, 1991

"There will be strong violent winds, storms across the prairies, in the towns. Violent! Yellow stormy skies, waves on the shore, high waves, high winds. It is a scene of natural calamity along the coastal areas. It is not (*globally*) catastrophic; it is humbling, and it is a humbling leveling action. It is not disaster on a grand scale but a disaster for many.

"It is not important. The land and the people will survive and continue with a renewed set of values. It will be beneficial experience, but the storms will rage beforehand. Storms, snow (*I can see snow*) out of season. People will run to the mountains, but the mountains will rock. It will all settle, it will become quiet once more, re-establish. There will be a new pioneering spirit form afresh in the hearts of brave and strong peoples. They are survivors against adversity; it is a strengthening of souls that had become flaccid and wayward. It is a salvation of souls. There will be born geniuses in that time. Men of special talents, men of clear sight."

And later during this session I received this: "The winds in America will blow more strongly than ever before. They are used to strong winds, but these will surpass anything previously experienced."

Possible Choice of Habitation

During one session, I saw that there would be choices as to how to live, depending on the prevailing environment. One choice was to live under domes, vast areas under cover. I was reminded of the Eden Project in Cornwall. Another choice was to live under the sea. There would be long tunnels leading to undersea cities. I believe something like this already exists but is secret.

The Moon's Eyes: September 10, 1992

I have a picture of the moon and of man standing on the moon, and the weightlessness and the dust and the craters that are seen as eyes. It is strange because I am looking at the crater eyes with the movement of the dust, when the eyes open like doorways, circular shuttered doorways with the shutters acting as eyelids. As they open, one can go to the interior. That is strange, isn't it? (I wonder if this is related to the suggestions that there are bases on the moon?

NB. I have a cassette recording of a BBC Radio 2 interview stating the existence of domes on the moon.

In 2020 I wrote in my *Calling Earth* trilogy about what currently happens on and in the moon.

Industrialization Taken Too Far: June 7, 1992

I can see in my mind's eye an expanse of industry, factories, smoke. It is an industrial scene. As I look, there is a great big wave, as high as it can go. It is rolling across as a wave of red, a wall of red that is sweeping across the land. Like a shutter of red being pulled across the scene, it is covering everything as it goes. The industrial scene can no longer be viewed through it anymore. The wave of red right way across has the quality of infrared, not a solid bright red. You almost feel you can see through it, but it is so difficult that one gives up the struggle to do so. It is as if you know behind it there is something there, but you cannot quite reach visually.

Out of this gloomy red step human beings. In twos at first, holding hands, an older and younger. As I watch and try to pin recognition on them, other humans are stepping out of the red, silently holding hands, in twos. Just stepping out of the gloom. Many are following and stepping out of this that has descended on them. It is a strange thing to describe, and I cannot identify but just know they are human beings stepping forward and surviving what has overtaken them. They are silent, no words, just two by two, not a great horde. Slowly but with a sense of bewilderment, with a sense of coming out of dreamtime and not fully aware of what has happened. They are dazed and recovering but with a sense of bewilderment and shock about them. They have survived.

I asked what period of time this was.

"It is when your industrialization has reached the pitch where it cannot be contained any longer. When it reaches explosion point and cannot be encompassed within the law of things. That is when this scene will take place."

I see mountains like the Alps with water almost up to the peaks. As I watch, the water freezes so that it is solid from the ground up, i.e., down to the ground.

Movement of Populations: June 11, 1992

I have a picture of dwarflike people, eyes that look at you as if every thought is known to them, telepathic. Now it changes, and there is a picture of people skating over ice, smooth ice like a frozen lake. There is no danger, for the ice is solid down to the ground. This is ice on land. I am shown what appear to be caves on hillsides, and there are people sheltering, bunched together, and trying to keep warm in the caves. I do not know if they really are caves. They are huddling close to one another, groups of people looking out at the frozen land.

They look bewildered as if they do not know what has happened. The sky is very dark, and it has a green tinge, a very unusual color. It is not a natural color. They have no provisions and have nothing but themselves. I do not know how they can help themselves. They must venture out and search, for they must not stay where they are. They will not survive if they stay where they are. I have a strong feeling that this has happened in the past, it has already happened before. There must be movement of peoples. That is what they are trying to say.

"There must be movement. One cannot remain in the same lands if there is to be survival. It is useless to cling to the homeland. Large-scale movement of population to areas of growth is essential."

As if to show an example, I am given a picture of people who live at the foot of a volcano and whenever it erupts they rebuild later in the same place. In this case of the caves shown, it would be stupidity; they must move.

New Thinking, Restructure: June 3, 1992

I have a picture of men tearing up papers and substituting others in their place. I can't quite work that one out.

"The papers are documents relating to scientific research.

Figures, calculations, and formulae long established will be replaced. A new thinking, a new direction of endeavor is required. The old conditioning will be swept aside. Restructure, there is to be restructure." (Of energies?)

I cannot understand.

"Restructure of both on a material and physical level. Genetically speaking there is to be restructure. One might say rapid evolution. Yes, indeed there will be changes which you cannot imagine."

I ask for a picture. I know it sounds absolutely crazy, but it is not the first time that I have had it, so don't laugh, will you? It is a picture of people in the air without any visible means of support. Oh, it is clear.

"It is a demonstration of ability to defy gravity—antigravity, you might say. It is not necessary to escape the pull of your earth to experience this and to utilize this in many ways for transport and other objectives useful to mankind. It has in fact been done before. This has been achieved in your past but was misused. It will be so again."

Global Change and Other Worlds: May 28, 1992

Somebody said, "We have got lift-off." I see a big television set, but it is a panoramic view like a viewing point, like a television screen without a boundary. All I can see now is a sea with a big swell on it, rolling. I can feel the motion. I can see the sea, and underneath the water I can see as well. It is like a cutaway view. Under the sea are mountains; I can see mountains below the water. As I watch, the water is stilled, frozen, a dead stillness.

A guide sitting with me and watching says, "Everybody thinks of the warming as being a raise of temperature. Consequences are not always so; the consequences alter patterns to the extent that there is a dramatic lowering of temperature not previously imagined in certain areas. A shift in position of temperate zones. Siberia one imagines to be an area of intense cold. That is a mistake, there will be a reversal. Those now wishing to be anywhere but in Siberia will gladly remain there, a land of plenty, of abundance, of pleasurable existence."

I see a land peopled by many; they are very short people. I see vast canopies, enormous expanse, enormous expanse of covering, manmade artificial covering over the land. I do not know if this is here (or on another planet).

"It is a means of existence elsewhere, perfectly practical and feasible. It is one that may need to be created for the continuance of life in certain areas. Environment!"

Talk about science fiction!

"What is fantasy to you is quite normal for those who live in this manner. Your method of existence to the eyes of many appears to them to be fantasy, a world in the imagination only. We who have communication and knowledge know and fully realize that there are many facets to life, as you yourselves are aware that thought alone is also an existence. There are many (worlds) that even you would find difficult to comprehend."

He is showing me squares and triangles and shapes in colors, and they are all moving about—everything is a shape of geometric form.

"That too is a reality every bit as valid as your own."

At this moment, a different tone of voice came in: "Note when the birds fly in. The birds know. The birds will take to the air in numbers and are directed. They have a sense of purpose and know their direction. When the birds take to the air, that is the time. That is the time for more than just communication. They will take to the air in numbers great. It will be noticed. That is when you should be aware of something to happen of relevance to the discussion. You will also notice an attempt to take to the air those birds that have lost the power of flight. The urge will be to take flight once more, even though it is physically impossible. This too will be noted. It is a primeval instinct that will surge once again. It will be so strong as to override reason. What we are saying is that logic will take flight."

It is difficult to receive this clearly. He is giving me a picture because I cannot find the words. There is somebody holding my thumbs. I will describe. All the flightless birds are struggling hard to fly, and they can't. I feel this may be symbolic and open to interpretation.

Waters Flooding Country to Country: January 13, 1993
I am being shown something, a picture of icy waters pouring from one land to the other. Waters pouring from one country to the other, flooding, not directed. Pouring, flowing, and carrying with it mud. All is washed away in the flood. Mud, animals, objects all washing along in the tide. I am asking where this is.

"In many lands, not just one, not just one continent. In many over the same period. Waters on the eastern sides, rivers rising and flowing backwards. Some will welcome the water; indeed to many it will be a salvation. It will be a renewal, hope that will spring again and cries of hallelujah. Waters will deflect the attention that is resting so heavy at this time. An order of priorities will be re- established. They will not be as now; it will not be man against man. It will be man with man."

Be Aware of All Worlds: February 27, 1993
I have a picture. How can I describe this? It is so difficult to put into words, and I am going to have to find my own words, though they are not adequate. I have a face looking down on the planet and the planet surface and the lands and the seas and then penetrating into greater detail individual countries, individual towns,

individual homes, individual families and people, still smaller down into individual pieces of anatomy, going still smaller into blood cells and so on and on and on all the way down into the smallest.

"Imagine how difficult it is to know that all that is there from a standpoint far distant. But know that you are recognized from afar, from worlds far removed from yours, from creations removed from yours. You know that you are recognized. Why then is it difficult for you to recognize us?" (I feel the reference is to existence of space beings.)

Primeval Swamps

I have someone with a silver head. He has eagle eyes, and the nose is like a beak. It is right in front of me, so strong. The eyes are looking so unblinking into mine; it is a joining of eyes. I can feel being pulled towards them. Into each eye, there is a picture like looking into a television screen. There is a lot of dust, swirling dust. One might almost say a dust storm, dry, barren, and dry hot winds; the sun is red, deep red. I have never seen the sun that red, as if it is not the sun. Enormous, it is extremely hot, and over the surface of the ground there are creatures, close to the ground like lizards. They are adapted to the heat.

"It is not everywhere." This came in answer to my unspoken question.

He flipped a coin, and the other side is steamed, wet. They are not merging; they are distinct. I do not understand any of this! There are no seas, no ocean.

"This is a temporary phase. It is not so long."

There are birds; I have just seen birds. I keep getting the feeling that it might not be our future. Perhaps that is just wishful thinking. It is the red sun that is puzzling me. Now I understand.

"It is what has been, but what was can return."

Thinking about the seas, I got the words *primeval swamps.* I do not know why they are doing this. They are emphasising a point of being and creation.

"We are putting things in perspective. You (*mankind*) have lost your sense of perspective in the overall pattern. You are too wrapped up in minor events. The perspective will make your existence much more understandable. It will produce a calmness and serenity and direction for each. If only the perspective of the whole was held in sight, there would be no need to kill, to envy, to seek after others' possessions. It would put things in balance."

It is the man who is also the eagle who is talking. The pictures have gone. He is the person with the long nose. He is like a magician as he keeps changing.

"We can use whatever means that will penetrate your mentality."

Floods in Desert: March 12, 1993

As I lie on the sand, all sorts of creatures are coming up to sniff me. There is a snake, not at all frightened of me; there is a little fox. I am an object of investigation and interest. I lie quite still so as not to disturb them. There are all sorts of little creatures here. A falcon comes and perches on my hand.

There is tremendous lightning in the sky. A storm, it is raining heavily, torrential. It is raining on the desert in sheets without ceasing. The downpour goes on and on until water begins to form in the hollows, which creates even deeper recesses. The rain pours off the rocks in high places. When the time passes, the water that flows over these rocks forms a lake in the depth below until the lake grows and rivers flow from the lake, permanent. The birds rejoice and come to drink and drop their seeds, and the greenery returns. It provides nesting, and life returns. I get a picture of a waterfall; the rain keeps on coming.

Prediction of Muslim-Involved War and New Lands Emerging: May 7, 1993

"*You must record this.*

The Arabs, the Muslims in the Arab states will involve themselves in the war at present in the Yugoslav areas. They will involve all countries where there are Muslims in numbers sufficient to unite. It will become a matter of pride and furthering belief in one's system. Politically motivated but driven by the feeling raised up in the peoples. Turkey will be involved, as will surrounding nations, and the funding will come from the Muslim states in particular the Arabs. This is for the record."

They are still with this.

"There is pestilence and contamination from sources out of Russia. Contamination that will cause many to fall sick. The contamination will hit all sides irrespective of religion or race. It is when the winds blow strong from the east, when the wind is steady from the east. There is much wailing, much lamenting. Such a cry as has never been heard before."

I am trying to pin it down. (I hope this will not be another Chernobyl.)

And later during the same evening's session, more came: "There are waters rolling over the land from the north. From the northern extremities, the waters will come."

They are showing me a picture of the water rolling gently, not a tidal wave.

"The waters rolling gently down are barely noticeable but inexorable and unstoppable. The waters will come from the north. There will be new lands, new fertile lands that were not in sight before. They will be a blessing when the time is needy. Virgin land, untainted, not plundered, and rich in soil. There will be a period, after the emergence of these lands, of biting insects. This will be a feast for the creatures of the air that will grow fat and prosper. When the balance has been set, this land will be fit for habitation.

"It is a period spread over time and is not sudden but a slow growth. These things are given to you, to give you hope during moments and long periods that we have laid out for you. It is not all a picture of despair and disaster. There will be in the final outcome of this stage a beneficial effect. Although it will feel lengthy and you will feel there is no end to the misfortunes of man, the dark period will not last forever, and the light will come again."

I have a picture. Well, these are searchlights coming *from* the sky and they are playing, moving about, and playing over the land. All colors, all the lights are shining from the heavens down on the land, and they are waving back and forth.

It reminds me of when you put a spoon into a pudding mix and stir it. The lights are doing this; they are mixing and blending using the lights. They are playing, and the light is going right through the Earth. It is not just resting on the surface; they are all penetrating the Earth.

Man's Construction—Wind of Change: June 4, 1993

I have a picture of a tower block. It is reaching up high so that the top of the building is in the clouds. There are hands on all sides of the block holding it up. I do not understand the meaning of this except the hands and the arms are supporting the building. Not just one pair of hands but several supporting the building, the dwelling places. I ask for clarification.

"So that the world built up by man, built by man and constructed by man, so that this world does not crumble and fall, killing all occupants of this constructed world, we are attempting to hold it in place. We are attempting to hold it together against the winds of change and the winds of force that buffet this construction. We are attempting to steady and retain in position until the winds have passed. It may be that our efforts will be in vain, but we are attempting to do what we can.

"You cannot see the construction above the clouds. It is lost from your view, but those who live in lofty places, those who have deemed it right for them to live in the higher echelons of your society, those who have decided that is their rightful position, they will not receive the same support, for the simple reason we cannot see into the cloud. Those who rise and put themselves in the higher positions would have the farthest to fall if their construction collapses. Unless they can fly, they would not survive the fall.

"We are doing what we can. We are talking of winds of change, winds that blow from a direction unknown to you, from a direction you have not dreamed of. You will not be prepared because your eyes are not turned in the direction from which the change will come. Those of you who have the sight to see, sight from within, will not place themselves in the dwelling places constructed by man's vanity. They will seek the open spaces and remain close to the ground from which they cannot fall. They will avoid the vanity of man's rise above others and above the creatures who cannot construct. Those men who have this foresight will not be crushed should the edifices crumble."

Golden Planet Force—Prediction? June 19, 1993

I have a picture of rooftops at night, and stars. It is quiet, and everybody is sleeping. I have another picture now. It is a golden ball in the distance, a golden globe, I should say. It is rolling, rolling is not the right word, tumbling is more correct. You know how you see an asteroid moving round and revolving? It is rolling along towards us

"It is beautiful, but it is equally perilous. It has a force that is natural to it, a force it cannot help but have. This force has an effect upon the surroundings and such things as are in the vicinity of this force. It is a beauty and a wonder but, at the same time, something which is not welcome."

I cannot understand that.

"It is the attraction, the attraction of the pull. A combining of forces, which is not in all cases to the benefit of both. It is nonetheless a thing of beauty and to be wondered at as a marvel. It is a portent. It is an indication of how change will come about upon your planet."

Preparation for Changes: June 25, 1993

I have a picture now of a lot of airplanes flying over. They are dropping leaflets, lots, and lots of leaflets.

"They are going a long way, and the cargo is full of these leaflets. They are printed in all languages, every language that exists. There can be no one who will say they were not told. There can be no avoiding the knowledge, even those who cannot read will understand. How each individual reacts is according to their own will, their own decision. There will be many who ignore, and there will be many who take heed. The messages will be broadcast also through the airwaves, through the television."

I want to know what the message is. How long off is it?

"Protect, protect, cover—do not run. You can conserve, disconnect, disconnect all amenities, all sources of supply,"— I am getting very hot. "protection—"

There is a wall so high—it is water—I cannot stay with that one. It was getting so uncomfortable and was as if I was there within that scene. A tidal wave I feel is referred to.

Bird Messengers Are Vital: July 2, 1993

I have a picture of a lot of birds flying over the ocean.

"They are flying from one land to the other, carrying grain. They are not only the messengers but also the bringers of new life. They will avoid the upheavals and will endure and be responsible for the seeding of the earth. They are messengers, providers for the continuation of life. Do not poison the birds of the air, for they are vital for your comfort. They are vital for the destruction of biting, stinging insects that will torment.

"You have need of the birds. You have need of as many birds as can be found. There cannot be too many if you are to keep the balance of comfort for humanity. Changes will produce insects on a grand scale. Pay attention to that which you put upon your soil."

They are giving me a picture of horses and cattle and various animals all trying to get at the insects that are troubling them. They are not showing people but animals. I think it is just to make a point. He is nodding as if to say yes. It is a strange one this evening. A show!

Turkey Prediction: July 9th, 1993

I have another picture. You know little fluffy chicks when they are newly hatched? I have loads of these little chickens.

Roy: They are turkeys.

Me: Are they? I would not know a chicken from a turkey at this stage. I am waiting for them to tell me what this is about.

"Turkeys make a lot of nonsensical noise, and that is exactly what is going on within the boundaries of Turkey. The events taking place are at the stage of squabbling, but the squabbling will develop into more serious irritation and anger when the biggest birds and the strongest will peck at the weaker ones and there is fighting one with another, brother against brother. The strongest will prevail at the expense of the smaller and less able. What appears to be innocent, even delightful grows into something more sinister and disagreeable."

I am getting the feeling to pay attention.

"Not that there is anything that you can do but to be aware. Do not be taken by surprise. Do not gloss over events as insignificant, for it is the insignificant events that will become the most important. So insignificant that they may be missed, except if you have a sharp eye and a quick ear."

An Inner Journey

October 26, 1997

There is emotion, a great emotion of—I do not know. It is the sort of emotion when one wants to cry, yet I do not feel sad. This is coming so strongly as if something has me by the throat—but it hasn't. It is my own feelings; something very deep, very emotional is about to happen. I can hardly speak for the tightness and ache in my throat. The deeper I go, the worse it gets. It is so hard not to cry here, but I have nothing to cry about.

I find myself on a flat piece of land. Open clear countryside. I must have been going down a hill. Where am I? I can feel the presence of spirit very strongly with me. Where am I to go? I look around, no clear path. There's purpose in this. I can still feel spirit very strongly with me, guiding my thoughts.

I see a whole city laid out, an entire vast city. But it is silent, nothing is happening in that city. It is like looking at the past. Only this is not the past that I am seeing. It is so quiet, no smoke anywhere, nothing, nothing, it is dead. No sound of traffic, no lights, no general hum that one gets with the city. Nothing. The tightness in my throat comes again. The feeling of spirit with me is stronger than ever. Why, why, is there no sign of life?

"This is the future that you are seeing, for one area of land.

This is the future that you are seeing."

"Where have the people gone?"

"Some are still around but are not there. They have vacated themselves elsewhere. Some were too late, for they did not believe."

I am trying to take this in. They give me time. I want to know about other places. I can only see this one place. "What about other areas?"

"It is a pattern which is repeated elsewhere. It is a pattern in many parts of your globe."

"Why am I seeing it? I want to know why. Why are you showing it to me?" My throat still aches.

"You can do something about this. You can alert men's minds. You can prepare them, give them serenity before the event so that serenity carries them through. You can do this. Give them the connection with their own souls, for this is what will carry them through. You can tell them this doesn't have to be."

"How am I to do this? Nobody listens to me."

"This is where your book comes in. This is how you must angle your book. This is the bias you must follow. This is the thread that must run through it. Give serenity to men's souls so that they may not be frightened. So that the calm they receive remains with them."

"It's not easy. It is not easy to reach the man in the street. How do I do this?"

"You will receive assistance. You will receive expertise, both physical and nonphysical."

"I'm incredibly pleased about that, but I have been told it is OK so many times, yet I'm still struggling. How much more, how much longer do I have to struggle with this?"

"This work is more important than all the other connections you have made in your life. This work has more importance than ever you would believe possible. Give people serenity in their hearts, not by telling them that these events will not happen but by giving them the strength to face them. Give them the strength to face even their own daily lives with calmness."

That is all I can absorb. I take a last look at the city that is dead. I look at its sprawling roads, motorways, buildings all silent. All in one piece but hushed. I look at it and begin to hear again the sounds of my room. I bring myself back quite deliberately. I can still feel them around me. I thank them for being with me.

New Zealand

I was in New Zealand in 1999 and was staying on the island of Waiheke. While there, I was looking out to sea at all the other islands. Suddenly, I saw that the water had vanished. I could see bare ground where there had been sea. It was a shock, and I noticed that all the islands were bare of water. Then it was back to normal again. Was this a sign of a tsunami to come or a rising up of the land? Only time will tell.

During a later channeling, we received this: "There will be movement, both of populations and of land mass. There will be strong winds. We know you have them already, but these winds will increase to levels that have not been reached before. There will be a rising of the waters. This you know already. This is already established by your scientists. We tell you that there will be mass movement of peoples. This should tell you that it will be a necessity, not just a desire. Climates that have been cold will become warm. Land that has been desert will become seas.

"Man will survive. Man will always survive. The great land-masses such as the continents and the inner parts of continents will be the places that are the safest. But there will be strong winds. Australia will be inhabited more fully than it is now.

There will be no restriction of entry into that country. Many of the small islands will become larger landmasses, for they will rise. There will be a change in the contours of land. There will be more water than previously. Mountains will fall.

"There will not be a comet strike. We tell you this for this is a question in the minds of your officials. There will not be an actual hit by an asteroid, which is what we meant to say. However, there will be a gravitational pull as a result of an asteroid. A gravitational shift as a result, without the strike. This is something to be grateful for. There will be—we try not to give doom and gloom. You see how we are struggling not to tell you all things. You have one on your planet, one volcanic interaction that is greater than you have ever had before. This will cause some disruption.

"Once again we assure you that man will survive. These events we tell you are not only because of man's behavior on the planet. Much is a natural event that would occur in any case. We ask that you focus on the quality of your soul and not be concerned over the condition of various countries. For when the soul is at peace and in confidence, then there will be no trauma attached to that soul. Whether it is reborn or is a survivor, this will enhance the growth of the planet, mankind, and that individual's soul. There will be signs before these events.

"By degrees, there are already signs that are being made known by the media—gently. Your authorities are already aware of what is possible, though they may not tell you. They are already preparing for events such as we speak of. There will be of necessity a unity between nations. There will be a ceasing of the constant economical battle for supremacy. Values will be readjusted. This is to the good. You might call this a new order out of necessity, a common goal because the economic situation of your world will be in disarray.

"So to lighten the mood (laughter), we tell you that this may be in your future. Carry on as normal and ensure the quality of your soul is on a good path. The soul cannot die. You will continue, as will the planet Earth. This change is necessary, for in its current state, we fear for the quality of life on Earth. Many of your species will survive. It is not the end for your beautiful planet.

"We in total have a vested interest in the continuation of the species and of the planet. We are able in combination to avert for you much of what is to happen. That is to say, if it was deemed necessary by a higher command, by a celestial command that we diminish, deflect, or make any adjustment to alleviate conditions, we are able to do this. We do have enormous power. We speak not because we are a galactic command but because we act under the authority of a divine source.

"We act under the authority of the Melchizedek, the archangels, the cherubim and the Elohim, and all those who have higher interests, interests of the highest and the lowest over the creation of your universe. Nothing is impossible. Events will take place on your planet so that humanity's soul may be saved. We are looking at the soul of man rather than his physical condition.

"You have the angels watching over you. They are present now. You may be aware of them. Those who like color may be able to pick their colors out. Each of you may interact with the angels. We feel blessed to be in contact with souls who wish to improve the lot of their fellow man. We feel blessed."

(Energy fading.) "We will now see what we can do to show ourselves."

It frequently happens when I channel, that spirits show themselves to anyone present at the meeting. What follows are the comments.

Tamsin: I can see you—gosh!

Juliette: You are a male form.

Tamsin: You keep disappearing.

I can see right through you (Shirley).

I see outline and the shoulders. It is twinkling. I am seeing ETs. Definitely ET there. Real big eyes, black—no hair. She is disappearing an awful lot. She is glowing from the inside.

There is a mist coming out of her.

Oh my God. Did you see that?

James: That is what I have been seeing all the time. ET. Big eyes. It is like that picture of Osishoo up there. Black eyes at an angle.

Tamsin: That is what came through really strongly, when Shirley was getting ready to channel. Oh wow! Did you see that light? It was going across there.

A different face there now.

Shirley: I shall ask them to go now.

James: You were disappearing all the time from the beginning, making it difficult to concentrate on what was said.

Tamsin: The angelic realm was there.

Hope for the Future: June 19, 2006

"There will be a good outcome in the world of yours. For there are many more good and enlightened souls than there are those who are non-thinking and profit seeking. The balance has been swung to the enlightened way, even if it is not apparent. What we say is that when the urgency is there and when all individuals feel that urgency to do something, then will they turn to prayer and go within and ask for help. When they ask, it will be given.

"There are many already in place on your planet to point the way, to point in that direction. Even those who have acted out of order, as you would say, even they will turn and pray for assistance. Help will be given there also. So you see, it is not as bad as you might think. But it needs to come to the point of urgency. Only when man feels there is nowhere else to go will he get down on his knees and sincerely and honestly turn to a higher source. Because man has and will request this, it will be given. If we thought that there would not be this turning, then we would be in despair, for the outcome would be bleak for the species of man and the planet Earth.

"Because we know that when there is nowhere else to turn, humanity looks to the divine and will have open ears at that time. It matters not what religion covers this plea, for all is one and all are included. Even those who have brought about the difficulties on your planet will seek assistance, and it will be given. All that is required is that it is asked for. There are so many waiting to assist when the requests are made.

"We trust that has given you some hope. We see the future ahead for man. We see far into the future, beyond your lifetime. We see a flourishing planet, a flourishing species of humanity. All will turn to order. So much help is waiting—so much."

I see a lot of fluttering lights coming down and settling. Like little snowflakes they look. They are settling all over in different parts, and as I zoom in more closely, I see they are angels and light-workers, beings of light. They are scattered all over and coming down and settling there when they are called for. A nice little picture.

Are there really big changes sitting there just waiting to occur? Perhaps, perhaps not but these are the more recent ones to be given to me. This one came in quite a different way on the island of Aruba. I was not meditating or thinking about anything but how to get ants out of my clothes, when I was strongly told by a voice to write. The energy in what followed was immensely powerful.

"Shifting sands, shifting sands. Smooth movement of land, vast land. Nothing is recognisable, nothing is left of former times. Move on, move on. The new is fresh, the new is welcoming you. Forget the past, forget the now. Look ahead. It is almost here. Can't you see it coming? Do not be caught unawares. Do not waste time. Get your mind settled in peace and readiness. The change is for you. You will do this with no company alongside except me. I am Ra, the greatest of all. Come with me. Be with me on my beam of life and you will know all."

This was not meant to be ignored and I wanted to shout it out. I have since included it into the new pack of *Little Owl Cards* as it is meant for all.

I am having so many indications that there is to be new man, a new human that I really took notice of this one that followed. It was the month of August 2014 given to me by spirit in the night. I will leave it up to each to decide if this is to be taken notice of.

Present man is dying and will die when the ice melts' Current man knows and accepts he is dying by degrees and that Mother Earth is killing him. she is waiting for the ice to melt. When it does he will die and she will give birth to new man.

The messages keep coming such as the one above. Often they come within a meditation and remind me of the style used by Nostradamus, ambiguous in meaning. At other times it comes out of the blue and I must write and let it come without any influence from my mind. If I oncc stop to think what I am writing, then it ends immediately.

Dec 31st 2007 **on Obelisks**

I have gone underground and am in the middle of a rough rocky, cavernous place, not closed in. Standing right in front of me is an enormous black obelisk. It is hard, black and some kind. It is big, gleaming and as I walk around I see a trench all around it. The obelisk clearly goes down into the ground and is not simply placed on the surface shiny. It is crystal of. The trench is wide enough to walk along if I wanted to. It is also quite deep.

"I don't know what you are telling me." I say to my unseen friends.

"There are many of these around the world in strategic positions. They act as – you might say as a tuning fork. Clearly they act as receptors for vibrations and in turn send out theirs. They form a link and are part of a grid. They have been placed there and have not grown there naturally. You will find one of these also in Brazil, though you may not see it physically with your eyes. You will see it in your mind and you will know where it is. You are being led towards it."

"I want to know why."

"When you find one of these in your meditations or in your most innermost knowing, meditate and walk yourself inside this grid. So as not to be on the outside, for there is an invisible field/shield that is formed when these link up. You need to be on the inside. Do this now with the one you have before you."

I am walking in what I perceive to be the inside, although I can only see the one. I seem to know what is inside. It is a huge grid.

This could possibly be an answer to the numerous obelisks appearing all around the world in recent times and nobody really knows why.

August 3rd 2018

ANOTHER PREDICTION? New people coming

I do not know what I am going into. It is a cave with an earthen floor. I am guessing that it is one of those caves that lead out to the sea. The steps have gone down a cliff, but inside the cliff, possibly used by smugglers in the past. As I walk it is sandy, mixed with sand and dirt. Quite smooth, easy walking. I can feel the air coming in from the other end now. Fresh salty air.

I see men with black rubber suits. They have clearly been in the sea. They are putting down some instruments. A receiver of some kind, square. I can't see much but it is some device, and I would say, heavy. As I query this I just know that all along the coastline these same devices are being planted in caves underneath the cliffs all the way along the southern coast of England. When the time is set they are all going to be activated. It is like a detonation. I feel the cliffs will be blown up or demolished in some way. I am not sure but there are many of these along the south coast going to be detonated. I don't know what is going to happen here. They are all in line with something offshore. The signal will all come from one particular point out at sea and they will all go off at the same time. It will cause a lot of chaos. It is a distraction; I do not know what from. My head is hurting so I know this message is coming from a source to be truthful. I don't know the purpose. I am asking for the purpose. *(heavy input)*

"Landing posts, landing posts."

"What for?"

"Easier access. There will be explosions. There will be landfall which makes it easier. While it may not appear to be so, it will be."

"Who is going to be landing?"

"New people to your shores. New people."

In meditation I find that if I query or ask a direct question I usually get an answer. Unlike when asked by spirit to write something I absolutely must not let my mind interfere.

I have had many other indications from spirit that we are in an era of change. There are so many that there would be no point in giving them all. The overall impression is that we can do much to help ourselves and that the quality of our soul is the most important factor. The soul cannot die. As if to emphasize this I received the following:

Your Future

We all have different futures. Your future is a potential based on your thoughts now. You become what you think. The mind grows accordingly to what you feed it and is unique to you. We are not all going to share the same outcome and we are not going to share the same future. We create our reality and that includes the future. What you believe to be true is your reality. We do not all perceive in the same way since we all have different viewpoints. What is your viewpoint? What are your thoughts? If you focus on the negative aspects of the future you create that future. Your mission is to focus on the great and wonderful aspects of a future world. There are some things that we are unlikely to change. Movements of the planets are an example. They are predictable. Your consciousness is not predictable - it changes as you grow with further information available to you. You all base your truth on the knowledge you have. Therefore it pays to expand your knowledge. Feed the mind with the thoughts and dreams that are good.

Chapter 18

One Thread Leads to Another

Whenever you meet new opportunities, grasp them with both hands. Don't let them go. Utilise all the forces for good that dwell within you and direct them towards these new openings. They will surely flourish and grow. The effect of this growth will spread outwards. *The Little Owl Cards*

Calgary, Canada: August 1996

The luggage carousel slid like a slow stream carrying bits of flotsam along with it. As I watched, my mind was elsewhere. Was I crazy? Most people would say that I was. This was Calgary. I could hardly believe I was actually in Calgary. I knew nobody; I had not come as a tourist, had no plans, and would simply book into a hotel for two nights. It was a long way to come from England on the strongest suggestion given through meditation. A retired single woman in her sixties was not exactly flush with money. If this did not show I had faith and trust in my spirit helpers, I don't know what would. Most people would say I was out of my mind.

My suitcase came into view. I reached over and yanked it off the moving belt. Now what? I threaded my way through the crowds towards customs and the exit. Outside, a wall of hot dry air hit me. I stood uncertain what to do next. Everybody seemed to know where they were going, except me.

A young taxi driver pulled up from the taxi rank and peered at me anxiously through his window.

"You all right, love? Where do you want to go?"

I must have looked even more bewildered than I felt. After a few words, my suitcase was in the back and off we went. On his recommendation, I chose the Lord Nelson Inn as my first stopover, until things became clearer. It was just far enough from downtown Calgary to be affordable. My room overlooked a shabby parking lot and, beyond that, a busy railway yard. I did not unpack but sat silent on the edge of the bed and let my weary mind go over how I had come this far. Why had I come and what did my spirit friends have in mind?

The signposts for my life ahead had been there all along. I just had not seen them. Just how far back did they go? Did it matter if I recognized them or not? Even writing this book had been clearly marked. How wonderful it would be if we could recognize the pointers through life as they appeared, and not with hindsight, as is so often the case. What mattered is that I now knew my purpose for living. I knew what to do with the rest of my life. Only the details were left for me to discover. Sitting silently on my own in an empty room across the world from my home was simply one of those details.

I teach meditation and believe that if we could communicate with our soul consciousness and retain enough of that communication to bring it back to our waking mind, we could learn much that would benefit our present life. Our soul has been around for a long time. It knows a great deal more than we could ever imagine. What is more, those guides and teachers who wish to assist us can communicate with our soul, who could then pass this knowledge on to our mind. All that is required is making that connection.

I was sitting in this stark and empty room because of just such a connection, an inner-state meditation. During that mind's journey, I had walked down a broad airport passage and came across a circle of Native Americans sitting on the ground.

I opened the contact with "What are you doing here?"

"We are discussing you."

"What about me?" I was not the least bit surprised. After all this was my meditation, wasn't it? Anything could happen.

"We want you to go to our lands."

"That's not very helpful. Your lands are all over America. You'll have to be more specific."

"Northwest," one said.

"That's still not precise enough." I said.

He pointed to a large map and placed a bony finger on Calgary. "This is a thank-you for a good deed you did for one of our kind." I wracked my brains to remember. Yes, I had helped a full-blood American Indian woman and her children in Italy some years before, when she was without friends or money.

My guides have never let me down, so I took up the challenge. So here I was in a foreign land. What now?

After unpacking, I showered, changed, and with some trepidation, left the hotel and set off down the street. One way led to shops and bustle, the other to the river. I decided on the river. Crossing the bridge, I came across a little collection of shops. It seemed homely, even more so when I discovered it was called Kensington. This reminded me of home in England. I entered a bustling New Age bookshop since I hoped to sell the *Little Owl Cards* that I had produced, the result of words given to me from spirit. They would serve as an introduction at least.

The manager John Hunt was sent for.

"My spirit guides have sent me here," I began. I explained the scenario of my meditation. The worst they could do would be to throw me out as a nutcase. There was silence for a few moments while he took it in.

"You must meet Thomas," he said at last and took me round to a little room at the back. I repeated my story to Thomas, who was eager to know more.

"You must meet John. He is in the shop, as it happens," he said and took me to meet him. John had amazing eyes that seemed to see into you.

"Before the week is out, you will give readings," John said. And so it went on. I was introduced to one person after another. A phone call was put through to the Calgary First Spiritualist Church on Sixth Avenue NW, telling them I would go there that evening and would introduce myself, that I was from England and had been directed there by spirit communication. It might seem amazing to many people but, just a few hours after landing, I had already contacted understanding like-minded souls.

I felt certain that spirit had it all in hand and I was not to worry. With not much time before the evening service, I said good-bye to my new friends and walked back to the hotel. Another quick freshen up and I was off again. It would take me a good three quarters of an hour to walk to the church, following the directions given to me. At no time did I feel afraid, yet I was walking alone at night in a strange city across the world from home. I crossed the Bow River again and arrived just before the service started.

At that time, I had no experience of spiritualist churches in Canada though I had worked in and attended one in Washington DC and in England. For those who have no experience of them at all anywhere, I would explain that the service is much the same as any other church with hymns, sermon, prayers, etc. The main difference is that the service is conducted by a medium, and at the end, a portion of time is given to passing on messages from departed loved ones. The main purpose is to provide proof that life continues after death and that communication from the other side is possible. Another important point to make is that there is no distinction between various religions. All are welcome under the umbrella of the one Divine Source. All are equal in the sight of God, including unbelievers.

These churches offer an enormous amount of comfort and help, but I prefer not to be restricted to them. Mediums working in them usually have a brief, simply to provide proof of existence after death but are generally discouraged from giving spiritual messages from guides and teachers. I suppose it is because it is difficult to prove the validity of these, helpful and uplifting though they may be. I was later to come across an exception to this rule in Winnipeg, where most of the messages were from guides and teachers. It was a wonderful time there with members of the congregation being allowed to pass on messages that they too might be receiving.

I was soon to discover that the church I now found myself in followed the usual trend. When the service was over, I hesitantly introduced myself to the medium, David Oliver who turned out to be from Yorkshire. I went over my story once more and quickly had a little group of people listening. The president of the church invited me with a dozen or so back to her house for coffee. I was later told that this in itself was an exceptional thing for her to do. Being extremely house-proud, she rarely invited groups to her home. My spirit helpers were at work again.

They were not finished yet. While on the plane, I had prayed hard for someone to show me around and introduce me to others and to cart my luggage to wherever I was needed and where I could have a bed for the night. During that evening's chat, it was arranged that I give readings at the church, that I give a demonstration and be the main speaker there while I was in Calgary. What was more important to me was somewhere to stay, as I knew I couldn't afford to stay in the hotel too long.

Present in the invited group was Syd, a gentleman who somehow had been included in the invitation to coffee, even though he had no connection other than he was doing some renovation work on the building. It was Syd who picked me up early each morning before he went to work. He took me around each day, dropping me off here and there to give a reading or healing to people he knew, and he knew plenty. At each place, I was offered a bed for the night as well as a meal. Only the second night in Calgary was uncomfortable, when Thomas from the shop kindly offered me a bed that I accepted, only to find that it was a hard therapy couch in a tiny box room. I stayed just one night.

I had a wonderful time and met a great many people. I'm still in touch with some of them and have been back a few times to work there. Spirit Indians knew what they were about when they gave me the suggestion to go to their lands. I'm glad I took them up on their offer.

Keeping Indian Joe and White Owl in mind, I told Syd that I needed to connect with the Native Americans. "Bragg Creek is what you want," he said. We set off, and long before arriving, he suddenly swerved the car off the road onto a track. After some distance, he pulled onto a patch of bare land.

"Get out," he said. For a moment, I thought I was being dumped since he stayed in the car.

"Over there is a memorial cross to the Blackfoot nation. You might like to see what you can pick up," he said. Looking around, I saw it. A white stone memorial surrounded by railings. I entered the enclosure and linked in. Very soon I saw a tall Indian chief in full headdress facing me from the other side. Two other Indians appeared, one on either side of me. They put a full headdress on me. The first chief walked towards me carrying a bundle. He laid this down at my feet and I saw it was a papoose with a baby in it.

Throughout the entire time, I heard drumming.

"Welcome my brother," he said. With that, he and the scene vanished. Still spaced out, I walked back to the car, where Syd was fast asleep.

I later discovered there is a strong energy field of seven kilometers from the centre point of this memorial which is called Lady of Peace. It is on Indian Sarcee land.

What comforted me many times while I was traveling and working in Calgary was the presence of Dr. Po. He was seen by so many individuals during healing workshops or during channeling in the church. On one occasion when he was speaking through me, a lady in the front row began to cry. When the evening was over, she came up to me.

"I have never seen spirit before," she said, "but I saw a Tibetan over you clearly. He then left you and came down to me and touched me on the arm. It was wonderful." She was so thrilled.

It was not the only time that he has left my body and gone over to someone else to comfort or heal them. He is still doing this when the need arises, and I'm so grateful for his presence. Some people tell me that he visits them at night or in their meditations after they had been to see me. There is no mistaking him for anybody else. Many times he is seen over me while I am giving channeled soul readings.

The Thread Continues to India 1997

I am in awe of the ability of the spirit world to set things in motion and to organize events so that you follow a path determined by them but unknown to you. I give this story as an example of what I mean.

I was again in Calgary, Canada, on my second visit there. A young man called Darren was introduced to me by the spiritualist church group. After a little exchange, he reached into his jacket pocket and brought out a photograph.

"Here, take this," he said. "I think you will find it helpful."

I now know it was a picture of Sai Baba, though at the time I had no knowledge of this man. Not wanting to offend, I thanked him and put it away and forgot all about it.

I continued my tour across Canada and down into Washington DC, where it was arranged that I stay with a friend and give readings at her place in Bethesda and at the Arlington Metaphysical Chapel. It was my intention to go round suitable bookshops and introduce the *Little Owl Cards* that were messages to all from spirit through inspired writing. Most of these were from the White Brotherhood and some of them are included in this book. I took myself to Georgetown and found a little bookshop there. As I was wandering around the shelves, the owner of the shop, an Asian Indian, approached me.

"I think you should have this," he said as he thrust a little book into my hand.

Surprised, I thanked him, and after talking about my *Little Owl Cards* and arranging a sale, I left. The book was the Bhagavad Gita, a story of Hindu teachings. I put it away and thought no more about it.

My guides had more in mind. I was working at Arlington Metaphysical Chapel on Wilson Boulevard and had occasion to attend a clairvoyance demonstration by Rev. Reed Brown one evening. On leaving, I was approached by a stranger who handed me a video after giving me the "hands together" greeting and saying *Sai Ram*. I watched him through the rear window as we drove away. He bowed, hands held together.

Next day, I watched the video. It was all about Sai Baba and the Dalai Lama. I was beginning to get the message. Again I put it on a back burner and forgot about it. On my return home, I had the usual list of people asking for readings. Among these was a family of Indians, the last being the head of the family unit. "Would you like to go to India?" he asked. "I have a friend who will accommodate you in return for healing."

It was too good an opportunity to miss. I would only have to find the fare, and the rest would be taken care of. It was only later, when arrangements were being made, that I realized where in India I was to go, to Madras, now known as Chennai!

I got out my atlas and looked it up. Staring me in the face was the triangle that made up Madras/Chennai, Bangalore, and Puttaparthi, the home of Sai Baba. Realizing by now that my guides wished me to visit this holy man.

I was tested during my stay in Madras/Chennai as it had its good and bad moments. The day of my arrival, my host, Manu (*name changed*) invited me to accompany him to his village. I naturally agreed, not realizing it was to be a three-hour journey, and I'd no time to change or unpack. It was close to 11:00 p.m. when we arrived, having stopped to visit several temples on the way. These were extremely pleasant stops, though I worried about insects each time we sat outside in the dark to meditate. I hadn't had time to change into long-sleeved clothes or to put on mosquito repellent.

We eventually arrived at Manu's plantation in his village. A meal was being prepared. It was past midnight when this was over. We ate in silence since Manu did not believe in unnecessary conversation. He gave me directions to get to the bungalow where I was to sleep, and he set off in the other direction. I had a torch, but anyone who knows me also knows that I have no sense of direction at all. I quickly lost my way.

I was in the pitch blackness with my torch, which only just illuminated dirt tracks stretching in all directions through avenues of trees. I didn't even know what village I was in or whether we'd gone north, south, east, or west of Madras. I was also still in the same clothes I had on when I left England over forty-five hours earlier. I heard a twig snap and a rustle behind me. Instinctively, I knew this was a test. I generally went around saying that nothing could hurt me no matter what. You could leave me in the desert with no water, I said. I'd still be all right. It was time to see if I walked my talk.

Irritated with my host for leaving me alone like this, I asked my spirit friends to send someone to find me. The precise moment I asked this, two boys came running up.

"Missee, missee, bungalow this way." They led me to it, and I went gratefully inside to sleep.

It was so hot I wore no nightclothes which were in my unpacked suitcase. I just pulled the sheet over me to keep off any mosquitoes. There was no fan, no air conditioning, and no mosquito net. When I woke next morning, it was to an array of faces at the glassless window gaping in at me. It seemed my bungalow was on the path from one side of the village, through the plantation, to the other. There were no curtains at the windows. I managed to wrap the sheet round me to the amusement of the spectators and made my way to the shower room. When friends say, "Oh, take me with you, or put me in your suitcase," they don't know what they could get themselves into.

I'd finished the healing work in Madras and was sent on from there by my host to Bangalore to stay with and give healing to a family who to my relief were an absolute delight. They arranged for transport to Puttaparthi. I said my good-byes to these lovely people and set off in the car for a three hour ride. The driver did not speak English, as usual. The ride was unforgettable. There were choking traffic fumes and vehicles packed in like sardines honking their horns incessantly until we cleared Bangalore. Then came the journey over rutted roads. There are extremely steep traffic "slowers," where one simply has to slow down almost to a stop and crawl over them. The entire ride was jolting. There were lots of monkeys and cows by the roadside. One sign said Accidental Zone, which made me smile. Spread out across the road is maize, for the traffic to do the grinding. Eventually we arrived in Puttaparthi, or Prasanthi Nilayam, as it is also called.

I spent three weeks there among many thousands of devotees, during which I cried a lot, meditated a lot, and read a lot. It was an amazing experience but not one I wish or need to repeat. I am not and never have been an absolute devotee of Sai Baba, but I do believe him to be genuine. That should have been that, but it was not to be.

In the years that followed, I heard him singing throughout the time I was giving readings in a house in Auckland, New Zealand. I could smell his incense while I was giving a workshop on Waiheke Island, also in New Zealand. He also stood before me in spirit and placed his finger on my forehead while I was in a group meeting in Minneapolis. There was one occasion in England when I was doing some housework, and I had an overwhelming need to meditate immediately. I peeled off my rubber gloves and rushed into my sitting room. I was told that Sai Baba needed me to do this there and then. I believe he does a lot of valuable work but that it is not necessary to visit him. As the years passed, I constantly encountered Sai Baba devotees and still do.

The connections made because of Shirdi Sai Baba and Sathya Sai Baba continue to this day. They have always been good ones and are most welcome.

Chapter 19

Africa Beckons

There is at times a need to take risks. If you always take the safe route, then your life's journey would become uneventful. Remember, nothing can hurt you except yourself.

White Brotherhood

Although this Sai Baba thread to India began in Canada, and continued through America, Australia and New Zealand, it was set move on to Africa. Shortly after my return home I had a dream. It was one of those clear, concise, "this is real" dreams. There was no doubt in my mind that the experience was a reality somewhere in time and place. I was upstairs in an apartment when a man burst in.

"Come quickly!" he said. "Sai Baba wishes to see you. Come with me."

Surprised, I mumbled something about not knowing Sai Baba was in London. I somehow knew this was London, and also that he did not leave India at any time. As it is extremely difficult to get an interview with him, I happily rushed down the stairs after the messenger and out into the street. We rushed past some railings and down steps into a basement. There was a crush of people in a long corridor, waiting to see the holy man. I was rushed past all of them and ushered into a room. I saw him sitting on the floor surrounded by a throng of people.

He looked up at me as I entered and sat before him. Grabbing my clothing, he pulled me close to him.

"You are to go to Angola to Mount. . . (*I forget*) . . . They have need of you there," he said and pushed me away from him. The interview was over. The messenger led me out and back into the street. The dream was ended.

Next morning, I went over the events of the night before. I realized that the Sai Baba I saw was not the Sai Baba of today but the first Sai Baba, Shirdi Sai Baba. I later described him to a couple of Indians, and they assured me that my description fitted perfectly.

The reality dreams continued. These are sometimes referred to as lucid dreaming. Next night, I was standing in front of an African village. Out of the village strode a very tall bony and well-built African man surrounded by maimed people. He held out both arms to me in welcome. I knew I was to visit this place.

A little later, during a group evening in which we tried to connect with the spirit world, he appeared. He was psychically seen. The description given by more than one person was exactly fitting the man in my dream. It would seem that I was to take notice.

It did not stop there. When I was in Minneapolis working and during a session with others like myself, he came again. The words *Kinshasa*, *a waterfall*, and *a mountain* were given. Not much, you might think.

My spirit friends continued to push the point home. I still marvel how they put things in place when they want something. I was recovering from a minor operation and feeling sorry for myself when the phone rang. It was an invitation to an acquaintance's home for a meal. I was more than surprised because I was just a casual friend and we didn't have a lot in common.

Shortly after my arrival at her home, I was introduced to

her guest, a man called Pastor Melo Josias. My host didn't know anything about what had happened to me in my earlier dream with Sai Baba or the tall African when she invited me. Since Pastor Melo was African, I told him of my dream and the details that came through our meditation links about Kinshasa. He became very excited and told me that Simeon Toko was the man I described as greeting me in my dream. His home is in Kinshasa. He knew without my telling him of the places I am to go to, including the mountain and a particular waterfall. He also showed me an article (*see Kindred Spirit*) about Simeon Toko, which depicted him as an avatar. This book is not the place to elaborate on this amazing person, but much can be found on the Internet about him.

I still have not been to Angola or the Congo, but Metatron has indicated that I will go when the time is right and "when he gives me the nod." In the meantime, I am to start at the south of Africa and move up. So far I have been to Kenya, South Africa, and Cape Town twice and Zimbabwe, where I gave a lot of healing. It was in Zimbabwe that I had my first ride astride an elephant. I loved every minute.

Africa does not leave my mind, and over the years that followed, I had several dreams involving that great continent symbolized in my mind by elephants. These too were real journeys that some would call lucid dreaming.

Dreams of Africa: August 26, 2000

Africa Baby Elephant

I have been drawn to Africa since I was a child. I read book after book on African adventures. These feelings have surfaced very strongly in me now I am an adult. It began with dreams. Not each night but frequently enough to be noticeable. In this dream is a baby elephant that I have enormous love for. I know it's a dream for the elephant gets onto my lap and climbs on my lap like a baby. I stroke it; I stroke its cheeks, caress it, and send it enormous love, for that's what I feel for this baby. I speak to it, and it answers me back. We all know elephants can't speak in our language, but I hear it. We hold conversations. I feel possessive of it. There are others who try to entice it away. There are film crews who wish to use it for their purposes to make a film. It is such a sweet little thing. There is another person who wishes to have it. I don't want to part with this elephant, for it's my baby. I stroke it and I love it.

I ask the baby, "What can I call you? I can't keep calling you baby elephant."

He says, "I am the spirit of Africa. I am the emblem of Africa, for where else can you find African elephants? You can find Indian elephants, but they belong to India. Here I am the African elephant and the symbol of Africa. I need nurturing and caring for. I need love."

I say I still haven't got a name. I must name it, for it's my baby. All the while this conversation goes on I'm stroking it, loving it, and sending it colossal love, deep heartfelt tenderness for this elephant that is suffering so much. It has only come twice so far in my dreams, for this must be a dream. And yet at the same time, I am aware of this reality. What does this all mean?

They want to take the elephant from me. The film crew want it. They want to make sensation out of events. But there's no feeling; there's no caring from them. It is simply for sensation and attention from the world, but not in a helpful way. Who really cares? Very few really care, but it makes good news. It spurs some reaction to provide aid, but it does not address the deeper issues, the hurting, the maiming, the killing that goes on. The help is superficial, surface only, and while these good people do their utmost, they can only scratch the surface. They have to go deeper to the heart of the baby elephant, to the children, to the core of Africa.

I come to realize that I am finishing my dream as the film crew try to entice the baby out of my arms and under the focus of their cameras. I awake out of this visit with my baby elephant. I must wait for the next dream, for it can only come and talk to me in this manner.

December 2003—another dream

I am at the seaside and looking over a rail at a small beach. There are people enjoying themselves on the sand and in the sea. Then I see a huge oil slick coming in. Swimming in the oil is a baby elephant struggling hard to keep its head up so it can breathe. Its trunk is waving as if calling for help. It is fighting hard to keep swimming and not be submerged by the oil. The people on the beach see the struggling baby elephant but are only concerned that they might get messed up themselves and dirtied. Nobody tries to help it as they leave the cove to find another beach free of the oil. I am amazed that nobody goes to its aid. I wake up.

These experiences are clearly about how we see and think of Africa and the nature there.

Chapter 20

The African Saga Continues

We trust that all souls unite in harmony one with another. Where a brother stumbles we ask that those nearby put out a steadying hand. Where one is weary we ask that a comfort for the soul that sighs is at hand. We ask that there is no fear in giving; either of your time or your possessions for all will be returned to you manyfold. This is particularly true for a loving thought, deed or service of longer duration. It is a promise to you that as you give so may you receive.

When you give to another soul no matter how black and dark the outer shell, you are giving to God for all things are of God. Be attentive of your thoughts and where they are directed for these too are received by God. Whatever you do, whatever you think affects the Life Force that is in all things, *yourself* included. You are not excluded from the Life Force in this existence or any other.
We as part of this same creation love you, watch over you and strive to unite you in the same joy that we experience.
Bless you all.
White Brotherhood. from the Little Owl cards

A Mind Journey

Tough elephant grass is all around me. I assume that where there is elephant grass there are elephants and I'm very nervous. I hear the crack of branches snapping. Imagined slithers of a snake close by freeze my steps and my mind for a moment. Lively small creatures skitter away from my feet. Sweat trickles down my back, and my shirt sticks to me. I pull it free it from my skin. Buzzing flies attack me from every angle and try to get into my eyes and mouth. An incessant high screech of insects fills my head while the pungent smell of droppings of large animals invades my nostrils. I stare hard through the bush, expecting to see something and yet hoping to see nothing.

I feel very small and insignificant, but this is the path I must tread. I weave my way through tall grass, too high to see over. My feet stir up clouds of dust, but the only sounds are the deadened thud of my shoes as I walk on soft earth. Dry stalks rustle in the undergrowth on either side, suggesting unseen creatures watching me. It cannot go on forever, can it? The grass runs up to and all around a clearing, enclosing it. From the edge of the clearance, I can see a round hut, typical of Africa. You would not know it was there from a distance, hidden as it was by the grass.

Now I see a group of huts. I walk up to the first one and look all around. No people there, nobody I can see at least. I stoop down and squeeze through the low entrance into the dark interior. It is very black. I cannot see anything at first, but as my eyes adjust, I notice two children on the far side, a boy and a girl. They are in front of a group of children all staring wide eyed in my direction. They are nervous of me, the stranger. I don't think they've seen a white person before. They crouch back against the far wall of the hut. There are no adults, just children.

I do not try to reassure them, for they would not understand. Instead I sit down cross-legged in the center of the earthen floor and wait. I wait for curiosity to get the better of them. A long, tense time passes. Eventually they struggle up from where they are huddled together and begin to come nearer. I see they are both injured. They were not born like that. They have been maimed. One is minus a foot, the other one minus an arm. They are not in good shape. They slowly edge towards me, eyes big and round. Because I do not move, they feel more confident, but are still nervous. I try not to look directly at them because it is too confronting. I look at the ground and watch them out of the corner of my eyes.

I wait and try not to breathe too loudly. After what seems to be an age, I slowly and carefully hold out my hand. I look at them and smile. They are still not sure. I keep my arm extended. The little girl hesitates but bravely stretches out to feel me. She touches my skin to see if I am real. She explores my fingers with an emaciated hand. She begins to feel me with more confidence and touches my arm and shoulder. Because I do not move, she comes closer and tentatively strokes my face. The smell of her damp skin and the dirt on her body wafts over me. The little boy watches and does not want to be outdone by his sister. So he too comes forward to prod me with one tiny finger. He soon becomes bolder, for he sees I am not going to harm them. He shuffles in a circle around me feeling my clothes, my hair and skin.

After a while, they both allow me to open my arms and give them a hug. I draw them close to me and rock their little bodies of skin and bone back and forth. They start to cry, a whimpering sound. Then they begin to sob. The sobbing gets louder and more heartrending, deep, deep sobs from the very core of their being.

I look up and find that adults are there after all. They have heard the crying of the children and have come to see what's caused it. They ought to be used to it by now. My mind tells me they are not used to it, for when there is deep suffering, there is no crying. There is silence and patient resignation, a state beyond crying. I look up and smile to encourage the men and women as they stand hesitating in the doorway. They soon come inside the hut, as many as can crowd in.

They see that I too weep with and for the children. I do not know what I can do here, except to be here and give them something from the outside world that isn't going to hurt them. This is a place that is not reached by the international aid programs. This is an area that is hidden and not reached by the outside world. I ask for spiritual guidance to see if I can bring some hope, some light into their existence by being their contact. I ask for the rainbow bridge that has been suggested to my mind to reach down to this place, and for it to be a bridge for the angels and to be covered with the light so that these children can cross the bridge when they wish. I ask for something better for them. The reply is that I am to take them when it's their time and lead them to the rainbow bridge and encourage them to go over it into the arms of angels.

NB: I have included this in my trilogy of *'Calling Earth'* since I feel it is of importance in reminding us all of the plight of many children who have suffered as a result of war.

I have had several interpretations from my friends about this experience, many of them diverse. Therefore, I leave it to you the readers to decide what this episode means. Whatever it is, it is certainly important enough for us to take notice. I was told during a channeling session that Africa covers a third of the land mass of the planet. If the whole planet is to evolve into a higher state, then Africa needs to be assisted too.

Teaching Children in African Village: Another Mind Journey
I am in a silver stream with little flecks of gold in it. I get out and climb up the steep bank. It is a hands-and-knees job. I hold on to tufts of grass so that I do not fall. I come to a hut such as one would find in an African village, a rather large round hut. As it's the only thing I see of interest, I go in. Stooping to enter, I see a man sitting on the floor cross-legged. He is not an African. I cannot see him clearly enough. I need to know who he is. His eyes are striking, clear. They look at me to the point where his eyes are the only things I notice. What amazing eyes! I sit down in front of him on a little cushion. He sits there looking at me, silently. A lot of children file in through the door. Children of all ages, little children, big children, loads of them, lots and lots of them. They come in until they fill the hut and are all standing around, filling every space they can get into. What is this all about?

He looks at me and hands me a microphone, a big one, the sort you hold in your hand. I would not have expected that here. This is very incongruous in an African village. I must call this a round house. What am I to do with this? He points to the children. They are my responsibility now. These children have traveled some distance from all parts, and I must speak to them. I must speak to them about what I have learned and what I believe and what the responsibilities are as a result of that.

He waits for me to begin. I tell the children to sit down so that everybody can see, even the little ones. The little ones must be here too. I teach them how they can listen to their inner thoughts, how each of them has a little being inside of them that they cannot see but can only sense and hear and know it is there to help them. I go on and on and on, giving them the mysteries of life, the realities of existence, and the purpose of existence. Encouraging them to know that each one of them is important and has a purpose in how the world is and how the whole of mankind behaves. It rests on each one, and they can all do something.

I can feel now a weight on my right hand. Something pressing heavily on it; I do not know what it is. It is on my hand, which is on my lap. Something or someone?

"It is in your hands now. It is up to you," a voice says.

How do I do it?

"The book must be the introduction. It must be the key."

There is something more, but I don't know what more I can say or do. Now he takes a map from his clothing and spreads it out on the floor so that I can see. He weights it down with stones. It is a map of the world. He turns to the children and beckons. They crowd round to have a look, and he points and tells them who must go where in the world. They are to spread out, and the influence of what they have learned must be spread all over. I am in the round house. I understand.

Does this mean that it will be the children, and as they grow, the adults in Africa who make a difference globally? Only time will tell but I do know that I am never ever given messages just for the sake of it and all have meaning. As always it is open for interpretation, but it is the reason for this book.

Chapter 21

Special Children and Parents

Soon after, I had another meditation, short but meaningful. Children surrounded me, throwing their arms around me, embracing me in a gesture of love. I felt their warm bare arms thrown round my neck, reminding me of my own children when they were young. Tears of pleasure came to my eyes at their innocent, unpolluted trust and total lack of fear. One could not betray a trust such as they had. As I was wondering if these were spirit children, a voice gently explained, "They are the innocent souls yet to be, trusting souls putting their trust in you to make the world right for them."

"That's a heavy responsibility," I said.

"It is the responsibility of those in the flesh to prepare the way for their coming, to give them a world which is not a hell."

The next moment, I was among a sea of new babies, all lying in their cots. They were perfectly happy, waving their arms and kicking their little legs. The whole area was covered with these new-born babies. A golden light appeared, washing over them. The same gentle voice as before began speaking, "They may appear to be babies, but they are more than they seem. They are the promise of a blessed beginning, each covered by and bearing the mark of the golden ray. They are each and every one marked with a blessing that is to protect them for their special purpose in their next existence. All children who are dying and leaving the earth at this time will receive the golden aura that is being bestowed."

I next found myself in a dormitory of sleeping children. A tall person in white was moving along the line of beds, very gently saying, "Come on, come on, wake up. It is time for you to get going."

He and others like him were shaking the children very gently from their sleep and saying, "Come on, get started now."

The voice came again, "They are not incarnated yet, but are to be."

I came back to my world. Why, I puzzled, was I fixing on children? What had they to do with my life? The only connection I had with children or babies these days were my grandchildren, and even they are now grown up. Anyway, I reasoned, the children in the dream had not yet been born.

The next night was sultry and heavy with the promise of a storm. All the windows in the house were open in the vain hope of catching a breath of air. I was still up although it was far into the night. All was quiet as if the land was poised, holding its breath, waiting for something to happen.

I waited with it, allowing my thoughts to play over the faces of unseen friends. My head began to fill with energy, which was the usual signal that something was about to happen. It built up more and more until I thought my head would burst. Suddenly Raman, my adopted spirit father, was with me, dressed flawlessly as usual.

"It is pleasant to be here, my child," he said soberly.

I almost replied, "Hello, Father," but checked myself in time. "How nice to see you," I said instead. I saw a twinkle in his eyes at this and knew he'd been aware of my first reaction.

He came straight to the point. "Let us explain about the children. You realize that a fresh generation is constantly entering your world. This is not new, of course. What is new is the quality of being and level of understanding that comes with these children. We wish to state that the coming generation, which has already begun to arrive, has a greater strength than there has been of previous times. It has been endowed with a better understanding and greater wisdom to enable them to overcome the obstacles that the previous generations have inflicted upon them. They will be in sufficient numbers to educate their elders, though this idea will seem strange to many, and there will be resistance to this. Many of these newcomers have been waiting for this moment in time, for they have chosen to be of assistance. The time is now."

I wished I had been wiser when I was bringing up my own three youngsters. If only parents realized how important it was to have a wider understanding.

Raman sat down but did not relax, his back ramrod straight. "Do not be dismayed by the murder of innocents, which is current in your world. Many of those who have departed before their time will return for a greater purpose."

I remembered the African children and wondered if they were included. Raman indicated the far wall. My eyes followed his finger, hoping to be going on another trip. Instead, the wall presented a picture of little flames spurting out of the ground, reminding me of gas jets being turned up. I was astonished to hear Raman begin to sing "Keep the Home Fires Burning" in a deep and almost tuneless voice. It was so incongruous that I collapsed laughing. It took a little while for me to gather myself together again and quieten down.

"What was the reason for that?" I asked, wiping my eyes and trying hard to keep a straight face.

"For the children, it is important that the unity of the family be maintained. Maintain the hearth and keep the glow of love within the home so that there is always a bosom to go to," he said. "The unity of the family is more important now than it has ever been. If you wish for mental equilibrium, then it is to the home that your psychologists should look. It is the disturbance in the structure and lack of continuity of family life that results in the ills of your society. We are aware there are many other influences, not least of which is the scourge of drugs."

"Sometimes the children are more disturbed when the family stays together," I said with feeling. I thought of my own experience, when in desperation my mother left my father. Life had been hell living with both parents, and it was a great relief when we left. I could not agree with Raman entirely. I looked at him to see how he would respond to my outburst.

"My dear child, I am aware that there are instances where separation is the lesser of two evils. We are speaking generally and say that if within the family unit there is all that is required such as love, discipline, challenge, and security in its bosom, then many of the ills of society would fade away. Challenges of life are always sought after by the young and they look for them first within the home. This is demonstrated by attempts to assert themselves, pitting themselves against the authority of the parents. Trying out their strength, you might say.

"If they cannot find challenges within the home, then they will seek them elsewhere, at times to their detriment. We see too many fledglings flee the nest before their wings are strong enough. They either crash to the ground or are snatched up by stronger and more able ones. Or they fly into misguided areas and are taught in ways that would not be acceptable on home ground. Too many fledglings do not have sufficient nourishment of character or experience of challenge before they are pushed out to fly. However, we do understand there are times when the fledglings can find no nourishment at home and so are forced to flee for their very survival."

From his face, I could see that Raman obviously felt very passionately about this. "It is time to educate those children who have been selected and who are already with you. They are to receive special attention, for they are wise beyond their years," Raman said. "They have come at this time on a particular mission. The mothers also have been selected for the education that we have in mind. We are not speaking here of the normal school curriculum, but of being made aware of things beyond your physical world. They should be prepared until they fully realize this for themselves. It will help them to have a proper sense of balance and order so that their full potential and purpose is adequately activated. Mothers have the main responsibility for this preparation. The rest of you who already have awareness beyond most of mankind are also to have a hand in encouraging these young ones. They need to be protected from ridicule and warned not to neglect the materialistic side of life. Balance in all things is required.

"These young ones will grow to become leaders and teachers. They have waited for this time of coming. They are the first wave, but there will be selected new generations to follow, to continue the work."

"Will we recognize these children?" I asked doubtfully.

"Your point of recognition will be with the eyes. There you will find a maturity, a knowing, and a natural kindness towards others. There will be a strong imagination and at times an absent-mindedness, a sense of being preoccupied elsewhere. They are to be allowed their time of daydreaming, for it is a vital ingredient for them. They should be allowed their periods of solitude, where no activities are thrust upon them. That is not to say that they should go into solitary confinement, but if they wish to be secluded for periods of time, then this should be allowed." Raman's dark eyes flashed with deep feeling as he spoke.

"I'm not clear about all this," I said. "Where do I come in?"

"You teach others, do you not? You tell them about life after so-called death, do you not?" he replied.

"Yes. I suppose I do," I answered, slowly catching on.

"The majority of your classes are composed of women, many of them mothers or grandmothers. Who better to understand the process we are speaking about? They can do so much for the world." As usual, he scratched his bushy chin while thinking. He stood up. "We will visit the viewing room again," he said decisively.

"Oh good!" I was happy at the prospect. Once more, my wonderful father figure put his large hands round my head. I felt the familiar pressure building up.

"Open your eyes," he commanded.

I found myself standing in the circular viewing room that was now quite familiar.

"Sit down, please," instructed Raman. His hand opened the picture.

A man's face appeared, one I'd seen before. I had called him Domehead because of his tall, elongated dome-shaped head. His eyes were clear green and very round and large. I felt that Raman chose which program to show me at any time. It was much as one would put a prerecorded video on. Domehead began to speak as if on cue.

"Those of you who have children in your charge or within your influence have a responsibility that goes beyond the bounds of normal encouragement, upbringing, and care. We are speaking of encouragement in imagination, in the realms of seeing within, or a practicing of sight with the eyes closed. Encourage invention of storytelling where the thoughts can run free and bring to reality by voicing the pictures from within the mind.

"All children should be encouraged in this. This information is not given for mere academic interest, for these young ones will be in a position of influence and leadership in times to come. They are to be prepared well."

I thought regretfully how little contact I'd had with my own grandchildren when they were young.

"Encourage compassion for those less fortunate. Encourage special insight when eyes are turned upon unlovable ones, whose deeds are not acceptable to the heart. Compassion must be taught for that which appears to be ugly, for this will be required. These young ones will be the fortunate souls, for they will have the strength that carries them forward, certain that they know the reason for their existence. They will know that the rewards will be great.

"However, we caution you to exert a gentle approach. Do not be fanatical as is so often the case with zealous individuals who feel they have a mission. There are many reasons for incarnation at this time, and not all are set towards the realms of service. Some have other matters to deal with in themselves first.

"Do not speak of it as meditation to them but present it as imaginative playtime where young children can perceive mind pictures and develop these into a story tale for their enjoyment and amusement. It can be done with the eyes shut or open, though one may say that more is seen in fairyland with the eyes shut. Children born at this time have chosen to do so for a specific purpose, particularly those young ones who are dying early to be born again."

I was having a hard time deciding how these new ones would be recognized. The method given earlier seemed too vague to be reliable. I needed more to go on. What were the events where special leadership qualities were required? As I pondered these questions, I became aware of the large, unblinking green eyes watching me closely. It was uncanny. My mind was being read. I shifted uncomfortably in my chair, trying to change position.

Raman, who had been very still and quiet throughout, turned and said, "Is this enough for you? Would you like to leave?" He closed the screen with a wave of his hand.

"I don't know," I said uncertainly. "It's not that I am tired, but I wish there was more definite information, something more precise that I can put forward as a valid reason for people to act. I know you've indicated dramatic political and disruption of nature on a large scale. I know that today's children will be around, probably as adults, when these things happen. But . . ." I tailed off. How could I get across to Raman what was bothering me?

"What you are saying is, who will take any notice of you without proof? Is that it?" he said sympathetically.

"Well, yes. I suppose that is what I am trying to say. After all, who am I, a nobody, to tell others how to behave?"

Raman let out a long sigh. "You do not *tell* anyone what to do. You present them with what you have been told and shown, to as wide a receptive audience as you can, and let them decide their own actions. You give them awareness of the possibilities and let them make up their own minds. At least they will have been told. Their own growth and future will depend on how they respond." I felt a little easier. It was not up to me to do more than advise and teach if that was requested.

Raman broke into my thoughts again. "Remember that you are not the only one receiving this information. We are training as many as possible to channel information through in various ways. The interpretation of what is given is dependent on and influenced by each individual's thought pattern. This being so, there will be variations. The theme remains the same."

He swiveled his chair to switch the screen on again. The green-eyed man came back as before. "You forever wish to know what is ahead of you, do you not?" he stated.

"No, I wish to know when what you have shown will occur," I said boldly.

"We cannot tell you when. To set a date upon the matter would provoke many undesirable reactions. There are many facets to be considered, many interactions from sources over which we have no control. The date may well be adjusted forward or backward according to the actions of mankind. The players are not yet in place. If all goes as intended and the will of the players is not contradictory to the program, then proceedings will take place at the expected time. If not, then there will be a reshuffling of events.

"Think of it as a plotting room such as you had during your last war, for movement of troops and resources according to events. Place this in your mind, with our team constantly repositioning, trusting the moves will have the outcome expected of them. If an unexpected event occurs, there has to be a new thinking, a new strategy. Can you understand that analogy?"

"Yes, I understand," I mumbled. It had been a long day.

"You need not be overly concerned. What is of importance to you is how you conduct yourself on a daily basis. Go about your business, follow your life according to spiritual values. It will be clear when we wish you to take a certain course of action. In the meantime, do not be precipitous. Consider where your actions may take you." He closed his eyes, for which I was grateful.

Raman closed the screen and stood up. "It is time to go," he said briskly.

"But there are still many questions in my mind," I said quickly, before he could return me home. I didn't want to go yet.

"What are your questions, my child?"

"It is to do with the children. You have given general guidelines on how to deal with their spiritual and psychic education, but I don't see how anyone can know for sure if their child is one of those referred to. Every parent thinks their child is special and cleverer than any other," I pointed out.

His reply made me stagger. "We are speaking here of genetic change as much as prior knowledge being given to them. That is, knowledge of their role will be made clear to them when they are old enough to make decisions for themselves. This awareness will come at an early age." He stated this emphatically and, I thought, rather fondly, as if he had everything to do with it. Perhaps he had.

"What is more," he continued, warming to his subject, "not only will you recognize these young ones, but they will ensure that you recognize them. They (their inner being) will ensure that they are in positions where they may enlist your assistance. They have been so placed that they may be in contact with minds that are already open to assist with the changes. Does this help you to understand more fully?" He delighted in surprising me.

I drew a deep breath, recovering my composure after the revelation of genetic changes. "How can I really be sure these are the special ones?"

"You will find that there is something in the eyes, a steadfastness. They will not avoid eye contact. They will also have a tone to the voice, hard to describe. We need minds to be more receptive and accepting of these differences without feeling a need for caution."

Puzzled, I asked, "Why should genetic change arouse caution in others?"

"It might make for a feeling of insecurity about themselves. It would be quickly clear that what is within their thoughts is evident and sensed by these new ones. It could be uncomfortable for some people," he explained.

"Are you speaking of telepathy?" I asked, remembering how easily the man with green eyes linked into my thoughts.

"That is part of it. We do not wish to put anyone at a disadvantage, nor do we wish there to be any anti-feelings out of fear towards these new ones. Therefore, we will not express the differences too fully at this time. They will be made known only to those we have trust in, those who will receive the information with gratitude."

"What about the parents? Surely they will notice the differences." I was getting tired now, but I wasn't going to stop. I'd show him I could be determined too when I felt like it.

Raman, the bright stone in his headdress gleaming, stared hard at me. He either hadn't noticed my energy was going or was ignoring it. I suspected the latter.

"The parents have been chosen as they always are, in all cases. The parentage will not be as you would expect. Some of these children will be born into environments which would appear to be detrimental to them, according to your standards. They will be placed in areas where there is the greatest need for them. Their qualities will overcome the difficulties, they will rise above any encumbrances. The parents are also chosen for their ability to encourage the child to develop inner senses and creative imagination, as well as spiritual attitudes towards others." Raman warmed to his subject.

"Some parents will have influence in the scientific or political world. There will be a mixture of environments, all for specific reasons. We are speaking of all areas on your planet, impoverished or rich, civilized or developing. Remember we have stated before that the mothers have been prepared on an inner level, at deeper levels."

"Do we need to find these families?"

"Do you not see?" Raman asked carefully. "You teach,

lecture, and write."

"Write?" I said, quickly picking him up. "What is this 'write' business?"

Raman delicately skirted round my question. "You may make it clear that children are to be encouraged in the manner we have suggested. If adults begin to understand the reasons and need for an improvement in values, then the children will learn by the examples set by adults. *All* children will benefit."

He changed tack abruptly. I realized he was very adept at bringing the subject round to what he wanted to put over. Answering my unspoken question as usual, Raman said again, "Do you think you can explain these things sufficiently to others?" he asked. "We have spoken about the changes to come on the planet. We require that as many as possible understand the continuance of consciousness and personality. These changes could then be faced calmly and positively, with hope for the future of mankind."

I began to see. "So, you want me to help prepare people by giving them the knowledge that whatever happens to them in this life, there is something more to follow, that there is something better, that it's not the end of everything?"

I looked at him, waiting for his reaction. I got nothing! He simply crossed his arms and waited for me to go on. "What if they don't believe me?" I challenged.

"Aha!" he cried triumphantly. "When you show others how to meditate and connect with their own inner being for themselves, they will receive all the confirmation they need."

He knew he had scored a point. I felt he rather enjoyed being challenged. He became serious once more and stood up. Facing me, he held out his hand, indicating that I too was to get up. "We must go. We have outstayed our time. You may not feel so bright tomorrow."

"Oh, do we have to leave?"

"Yes, we do," he said bluntly. He took my hand, and the next thing I knew, I was alone in my chair back home.

Chapter 22

Enter Osishoo—Time and Space

> Eyes that you do not see are upon you. Every move is noticed. When your actions are to assist someone else, Angels' eyes light up with joy and delight. Then *they* know that all is not lost upon the planet Earth and the heart is lightened.

All through the following week, I looked closely at every child I came across, to the consternation of some parents. Finally, I decided that I was going about it the wrong way. I'd let time take care of things. I settled down to routine matters once more and put all thoughts of children out of my mind.

Later that evening, after a warm relaxing bath, I sat and waited for contact. The clock on the wall ticked on, marking time as usual in an otherwise silent room. I knew I was not alone and waited while the pressure built up. Soon I heard Andreas's soft gentle voice.

"Please get up. We are going to visit the life-support system."

The memory of the floating platform came back sharply. Pictures once seen are never forgotten, they had said. They were right. "Get up," Andreas urged again.

I rose from my chair, still thinking of the floating platform, and squeezed my eyes shut. All at once I was inside. How, I neither knew nor cared. Before me I saw a semicircle of what appeared to be computers. Sitting at these were little people with large bald heads. I thought at first they were wearing round helmets, until one of them turned round.

Large, unblinking, clear green eyes fastened on me. Identical eyes to the one I'd called Domehead. The owner of these eyes had an almost non-existent nose and a small mouth. He was dressed like the others, who were all wearing tight-fitting silver suits, like a uniform. He turned back to his monitor and ignored me. I breathed a sigh of relief. I felt rather foolish standing there and wondered what I should do, when Andreas appeared at my side.

"They are simply controllers of the system," he said softly. "You are here to meet someone. Be prepared for the unusual."

That's a good one, I thought. Everything that had happened so far was unusual.

Andreas took my arm and guided me through a high doorway. I blinked in disbelief. Standing before me was an amazingly tall *man* with silver shining head and an incredibly strong face. What really held my attention were his eyes and nose. I could almost swear he was an eagle, not a man at all. He had a broad, downward-sloping proboscis, somewhat like an oversize, broad bird beak, with the mouth underneath the beak. He had a graceful ovoid head and a long thin neck. His dark eyes swept round his head. I knew he was telepathic and kindhearted.

My heart beat wildly as I was swept by a turmoil of emotion. I had instant recognition, a flash of knowing so intense that it shot right through me like an electric shock. I tried to speak, but no sound would come. My whole being screamed, "I know you; I know you, I know you" over and over again, but I stood there with my mouth hung open.

After a while, I recovered my wits enough to close my mouth. “Birdman,” I thought. That is what he is, a birdman. His presence was unbelievably strong. Entranced by his far-reaching eyes, I sensed he had come into my mind, amplifying it, stretching it. The energy from him was so powerful I could feel it tingling in my hands and arms. It was only when Andreas touched me lightly on my shoulder that I realized Birdman was speaking.

From his mouth, which did not appear to close, came a gentle whooshing, swishing sound, reminding me of the wind. I knew he was talking to me and telling me his name. The closest I could get to human language from the beautiful rushing wind notes was *Osishoo* (Oss-sisss-sshoo). I repeated it as best I could. Deeply moved by the unimaginably beautiful sound that came from birdman Osishoo, I wept.

Andreas lowered his head and whispered in my ear, “Open your mind. He will speak to you through your mind.”

I looked at the towering figure and realized he was aware

of my every thought. Comfortable with this, I knew there was nothing that I would not share with him. In an odd way, I knew he was already a part of my being. He began to speak in my head. At first it was difficult. The words came haltingly, as if the difference with mouth structure created a problem, even though he was transmitting mind to mind. I realize now that it was my own inability to receive that made it difficult for him.

"You will stay with us for a while, for we have much to say," he began.

"It is all right," said Andreas. "You are now adjusted. Time and space have been arranged."

They were pretty sure I would come. I wondered how it had been arranged. It was all right, if Andreas said so. I trusted him through and through.

Osishoo transmitted slowly. "I am not of your present race," he said, rather obviously. "I am detached, an observer. I notice the efforts of men being made in all parts of your world. The word must be spread. We are all observers and know what is required for all unopened minds and untouched parts of your globe. Word must be spread from one part to another, like a relay. You must use your mind, you must send your messages through the airwaves, through your electrical connections. Use satellites. You can reach all parts through a network of transmissions. Network, linking, many languages."

"Are you speaking of television?" I dared to ask, in my mind. (*NB). This was before the Internet. I later realized that if he had referred to the Internet, I would not have understood.*)

His eyes held mine. "You of the Earth are to keep in mind the concept of goodwill one to another. That is the basis of unity, making one harmonious conglomerate of souls. You must exist in harmonious vibration. If the vibration is out of tune, there is a jangling, an oscillation which upsets the vibration of all others in contact with it. You must work in harmony, one with the other. It is important to love your fellow man."

I reflected that this concept was not new. Surely I hadn't been brought here just to be told that?

"Shush!" admonished Andreas, even though I hadn't spoken.

Osishoo's eyes flickered, and I felt it. I actually felt it. "With love one for another, there will be harmony, smooth musical vibration notes which in turn will be in harmony with vibration notes of other worlds."

Now it was getting interesting! Other worlds! Wow! I sat up and took notice.

The dark eyes flickered again, and again I felt it. He drew himself up even taller, making me realize how tiny I was in comparison to him. "It is vitally important for the other worlds that the vibration they touch does not upset their own vibration note. Music must be in harmonious balance, or there is discordance, which travels through to the vibration of others making it difficult to set in balance." The words came with great emphasis, but it was apparent he was not used to formulating them.

It was clear to me that this was indeed very important to him. I felt his deep concern over getting his message across and hoped I would understand it by the time he'd finished. All those around us were listening intently, including the bald-headed controllers.

"We are anxious that the root of the discordance be balanced. We go to the root of the trouble, which is the vibration discordance on the planet Earth. You must attempt to influence those who are creating the discordance. It is not an easy task."

"An impossible one," I told him bluntly.

"If it cannot be done, we will have to influence you on the planet in other ways."

I felt the power and obvious authority this birdman held. I did not doubt his ability one iota. My mind was still held by his.

"The planet will continue as it must continue, for all our sakes. You are being influenced, many are being influenced. It is important to you and us that this influence is made. It is not for your sakes alone. It is for the whole of creation, by which we do not mean the planet Earth alone, which is but one sector. We are trying very hard to influence the minds of men. The balance will be made, one way or another."

(There is a taped recording of this interchange.)

I felt him release my mind as the communication ceased. We stood face-to-face with no discomfort, just total ease with each other. There was no need for words.

Andreas touched me on the arm. Dear Andreas. I'd almost forgotten him in my fascination with Osishoo. He didn't seem to mind.

"You will stay here until everything is transmitted. You will not be allowed to wander where you will. I hope you do not mind. There are radiations here which would not be good for your structure," he said. "Come with me."

I followed him through an opaque glass door into what appeared to be a sealed dome-shaped room.

"This has been prepared specially for you," he told me tenderly. "Everything you need is in this panel. Press this and a list of anything you require is lit on the panel. Press the appropriate button, and it will be provided through the chute. The bed is over there. I am truly sorry you cannot go beyond this area alone, but it really is for your protection. Sleep well."

With that, he left. I noticed his glow was even brighter here. How lucky I was to have him!

I experimented with the supply panel until I understood it. I couldn't settle. Thoughts buzzed round and round in my head. Andreas had told me to be prepared for the unusual, but I hadn't expected anything quite so startling. I began to feel the weight of responsibility upon me. I knew I hadn't been brought here lightly, something was expected of me. Serves you for making a pledge to serve, I mumbled as I dropped off to sleep at last.

Soft pastel lights playing over the walls and gentle chimes woke me. I presumed it was morning but had no idea of time. I freshened up, ate breakfast by courtesy of the panel, which indeed did have everything. Andreas arrived fairly quickly after that. He was quite clearly to be my escort and guardian during my stay. I was grateful. The experience would have been rather unnerving without him.

"The second session is to begin shortly," he told me hurriedly. Osishoo is apparently not one to be kept waiting, I thought.

"It is not that," answered Andreas, responding to my thoughts.

"There is a movement planned where the timing is critical. It has nothing to do with your visit, but we are trying to fit both events in."

We entered the room to see Osishoo surrounded by the bald-headed people, all very busy. He saw us arrive and waved the controllers away. We were alone with him. I wished he would hug me in greeting. I felt the need for physical contact with him, but it was not to be.

His eyes once more fixed on mine and held me. I knew he was about to communicate mind to mind. "One day," he promised simply. He beckoned to us to sit.

"To business," he began. "Know that all on your planet are recognized from afar, by worlds far removed from yours. We have something of value to offer, something that will be of benefit to all. First we must conclude our message regarding vibration coming from your planet. Remember the satellites. They should provide the means to further goodwill, thereby correcting the imbalances that are creating the disharmonious vibration we have referred to."

He became very intense. His shining head gleamed like silver as he tried hard to stress the importance of what he was saying. "We are referring to the shift in your weather patterns which are upsetting the polar regions. If this is not corrected, there will be a shift which will create mass upheaval."

I frowned. "How can we correct this? I don't see how we can control the weather. It doesn't make sense."

"Vibration note!" he said briefly. "There must be harmony in all things. Earth is not in tune with vibrations beyond your universe. We repeat, utilize your satellites and broadcast. Airwaves can reach all parts of your globe, all languages."

"I still don't see how or what we should broadcast, or how it would make a difference," I repeated. "If I'm to do something with your message, I need to understand." The large warm eyes flickered.

"I want to understand, really I do," I said desperately.

Osishoo's chest swelled visibly as he drew in a huge breath. "All languages can be affected by thought. Thought is very significant. Concentrate on thought patterns. Ways of thinking must change. Think of behavior towards one another. View your existence as a continuous one, forever and ever. Think beyond your material comforts. Think of your relationships with each other. Only when these are in harmony will the vibrations be in tune and will not create fractures.

"Vibration is extremely powerful. Your scientists will tell you that. It can destroy or make growth. Think how your physical body takes a sickening lurch when someone directs anger at you, or how your heart plummets when a loved one deserts you."

Oh, I remembered that one all right.

"The vibration of those actions quite literally affects the structure of your being. If this is continued over a period, your body becomes damaged, maybe it will even die. Now take this to a global level, and you can see how the action of mankind has a physical effect on the planet. Discordance is fracturing and breaking up the structure of your planetary home." He paused while I absorbed his words. He blinked slowly, which had the effect of increasing the energy in my head.

He showed me a picture of an organ in a church.

"There is a reason for such a large instrument in an area of limited space. The vibrations are greater and touch on all who are in the path of the waves of sound and whose very structure is changed by this sound. In being changed, one's own vibration is altered and your waves in turn spread out and affect other beings, other objects and so on and so on. It is not for nothing you have the expression 'that strikes a chord'. It is the vibration of what you hear or even think that strikes a vibration of the thought within and so that sets the chord twanging to produce its own wave of vibration. It is a simple analogy and there is far more that we could give you. Every sound, every movement produces a note both heard and unheard. What is not perceived by the human ear is perceived by others, by other living forms, by other material forms. It is all perceived, received, affected and in turn the vibration is carried on. So you see, harmony, harmonious notes as we have said is vitally important if there is to be harmony in the universe and beyond."

"I understand what you have said, but what can I do about it? How will simply knowing this have any effect on the weather or the changes you have indicated?" I asked.

"You become what you think. Your world is how you think it to be," he replied. "Thought is extremely powerful, as we have said so often. You can mentally create the ideal world where there is no war, no famine, no hate, no envy, no neglect of safety in nuclear establishments, and so on. There is no end to the possibilities for improvement of your existence. You can unite with other like-minded souls to work for the betterment of your world, through direction of thought. Thought has an energy which is powerful in its effect. Where you have a mind, you can put your thoughts into positive action by means of letters to those in positions of influence anywhere in the world. You do have a voice."

I persisted, "And the weather?"

"Ah yes! The weather. Ecologically speaking, man is having a disastrous effect in this area. You are surely aware of this. A chain reaction is inevitable if the irresponsibility of some nations is not checked. I will say no more."

It was true, I reflected, that the governing powers were already aware of what they were doing and preferred to ignore it. Commercial concern was a greater power than conscience.

I was just warming to the subject. "Is that where thought participation comes in?" I asked.

"Yes. If man believes he continues to exist forever and ever, that he will experience the consequences of his actions and thoughts, he will be more careful and act for the good of all. This will obviously benefit the total environment. What we are giving is warning so that man may take responsibility for his actions or inaction. It is not our task to dictate what he must or must not do. We merely give direction.

"It is said that an alcoholic must want to change before he can abstain, if there is to be a complete reversal of behavior. If dictated to, he will simply revert at any given weak moment. So it is with mankind. We have stated that changes will be made.

"The Creator, God, is often asked why he permits such distress on Earth and does nothing about it. If he did wipe away all your troubles, how long would it be before man reverted to his old ways? It is up to mankind to change its ways for permanent benefits."

Osishoo shook his silver head from side to side and blinked several times. "We will rest for the present. I will see you later," he said briefly.

Andreas took my elbow and led me gently out. As I went, I looked back at the impressively powerful figure, already engrossed in discussion with the dome-head creatures who had returned to the room.

"Stay with me awhile," I pleaded as Andreas turned to leave, having returned me to my sealed room. "There are questions I want to ask—where are we exactly?"

"We *are* on a ship. This is a space station, not the same as NASA has. This is a space station for traveling inter-planetary beings. That is to say, not from just one planet but many. It is a way station. Some might call this a mother ship, but it is not just that. It is a way station, a stopping-off point, embarkation for passages of interplanetary travel."

"Why the close-fitting silver space suit that you and I seem to be wearing?"

"This has properties that make it easy to enter the various chambers we have on board here. To a variety of systems that you might call 'airlocks.' They are adjustment chambers for different species from other planets. Each one (chamber) is different from the other and is relevant to the species requiring an interchange, a preparation. The suit that you wear enables you to enter any one of these without harm, for you too are a species that cannot always interact physically with all or any of the others. Not all are giving off the same energy waves, emanations, and radiation. So adjustment must be made before they can enter the rest of the ship or travel as they are here to do. This is why it is called a way station and not a mother ship."

"I don't quite understand how this works. No doubt you will tell me at some point."

"You might call them decontamination chambers, for not all the waves, the energies, the attachment in terms of physical emanations are compatible with the environment they wish to visit, such as that of the Earth. There has to be a decontamination process to avoid contaminating Earth itself or any others it might meet. If we didn't do this, there might be effects upon the flora and fauna and living beings. The energies are not always compatible. This is why we have a decontamination process in these chambers. We have chambers allocated to each species from certain regions of the cosmos.

"The suit that you and we all wear when we engage in this work is impervious to the energies from a whole range of species from other planets. We are not adversely affected by the varieties that visit this way station.

"These questions! You do not feel you can ask Osishoo?" he said.

I looked at him sharply. I hadn't told him the name I'd given the silver-headed Birdman. It was clear that he too had all the content of Osishoo's thoughts passed through his mind.

"We are all of one mind," he said gently. "What else do you wish to know?"

"I don't know how to put this," I replied, hesitating. "Is he real? I mean, is he physical or in spirit?" I turned red with confusion and embarrassment. "You see, it's difficult to know what's real and what is not."

At this Andreas burst out laughing until I thought he would never stop. He wiped his eyes and tried to compose himself. "We are all real," he said, trying to keep a straight face. "I am just as real as you. Everyone you meet and everywhere you visit is real and exists as much as you do. The difference between us is in the vibration and dimension of time and space. You have used the mind to cross the boundaries. That is all."

"Do you mean I am only here in the mind?" I asked.

"Your existence and reality is where your consciousness is. Osishoo is real. By that I mean he is physical, incarnate." Andreas said as he smoothed his suit with his hands.

"And the others, the bald-headed ones? Are they incarnate too? Is this place we are in a physical reality too?"

"Yes. Look, why don't you have a drink and stop getting so excited?" he said, pressing one of the panel buttons.

I waved the glass away. "Then, this is a UFO, and they are ETs."

Andreas raised his eyes to the ceiling. "We prefer not to use the expression UFO. As far as we are concerned, it is not unidentified, it is a vehicle for traversing time and space."

I wasn't satisfied. "Just a minute. You are not incarnate. Nor is Dr. Po, or Raman or the others. I know that much."

"How do you know? Do not forget time. I cross time." He smiled sweetly, the glow from him grew brighter and suddenly he was gone, leaving me confused. Surely physical beings cannot appear and disappear at will?

It had been an exciting morning, and I was ravenous. I investigated the supply panel, ate well, and fell asleep on the hard bed. When I awoke, I amused myself by waving my hand over the walls to see what I could operate. Andreas returned as I was engaged in this. He smiled, amused.

"How are you feeling?" he inquired politely. "May I sit down?"

"Please do." I offered him a drink. He shook his head. "You forget I may not be physical at this time." His eyes twinkled merrily.

"There you go again, confusing me," I said with good humor.

"I will be serious now and try to explain some of your queries to you before we join Osishoo."

"What about the others, Raman and Dr. Po? Are they—?" I quickly checked myself for I almost said "real" again.

"They are both incarnate and spirit, if that is what you mean," he said, chuckling.

"From your own *current* standpoint in time, they are in spirit but are no less real for this. May I remind you that you have already visited other times? Were those you met then any less real to you than those in your present life?"

I had to admit that not only were they real to me, but I was also able to exist with them as if I had always been present in their time. Andreas wrinkled his brow and gazed upwards, seeking inspiration.

"Let me clarify further," he said at last. "When we visit you in your home and remain there with you, we are visiting your time zone, and so appear to be spirit beings. When we take you to other scenes, other times, *you* are the visitor in those time zones. You and we are 'real' in all cases, for reality is where the consciousness is.

"But I don't think you quite understand yet. Let me put it this way. Someone in Australia is living, eating, talking, etc., but as far as you are concerned, he is in another time and zone. The same goes from his standpoint of time. If you telephone him, you can communicate, even though you are speaking from different time zones. Neither of you would deny that the other exists. Do you agree?"

I began to get the picture.

"All you need to do is expand the concept, for there is no limit to expansion in time or space. Naturally over longer periods, you leave the body and go to spirit form only, as you will do at the end of this current life span. Providing you have the means, you may still communicate with each other. In most cases, this is where training and meditation comes in." Andreas beamed, well satisfied with his explanation.

"We have to leave it at that for the moment. Osishoo is ready." He led me out of my confinement.

We entered the control room where I had first met Osishoo. He was in deep discussion as usual. While we waited, I looked at the tall impressive figure with new eyes. If he was physically present from another time and I was physically present too from my current lifetime, that must mean that he was from another planet. Why was he different from the dome-heads? My mind buzzed with questions.

Andreas looked at me, mentally cautioning me to hold my questions till later.

Osishoo turned around to greet us, his silver head gleaming. Once again I received the shock of recognition. The strength of it was both disturbing and wonderful, and I knew he felt it too. Once more I longed to touch him but dared not.

"Good afternoon, daughter," he said warmly through my mind. His eyes pierced my being. "Let me ask you a question," he began. "Would you agree that you are not alone in working for the common good of man and that the spirit world is also engaged in this effort?"

I nodded. Why didn't he come right out and say what he had to say instead of putting questions to me?

"Then it should come as no surprise to you that we of other spheres also work together with the spirit world for the benefit of others. After all, we do have an interest in mankind." He blinked his eyes slowly several times. He waved for chairs to be brought for us. The dome-heads obeyed.

"Why? Why do you have an interest in us?" I flashed across to him.

His face showed the nearest thing to a smile I could imagine. He was pleased with the interchange between us.

"My daughter, we have a part to play in your future, for you are our future as we are yours." He waited for this astounding declaration to register.

"You have also been in our past," he continued. "Many of you have experienced our world at other times. We do not have your precise form, though we are not so very different. It is not that we are like you, but that you are like us. We are all humanoid."

I found it was all very difficult to grasp. From what he was saying the past, present, and future were all connected with each other as far as progress for all planetary beings were concerned. It was small wonder they were interested in planet Earth and humans.

Osishoo watched me as I grappled with the implications. "In considering you, we are considering ourselves also. It is not a concept which is easily acceptable to man. You will be of the future as we already are. If only out of self-interest, you would do well to reflect upon this. As you do, you will come to understand that a love for your fellow man will indeed be a love for yourselves. You are of the future, the present, and of the past. This applies to every being."

Once more there was a pause as a dome-head brought something for his attention. I watched as they communicated through a series of whistling and clicking sounds. It all sounded very musical and pleasing to the ear. Lights from the consoles and switches were flashing all around us. I looked at the floor and noticed that there was no noise when walked on although it was not carpeted. I assumed it was covered with a kind of floor cushioning. I looked round at Andreas close by, grateful for his presence.

Osishoo uttered a swishing sound, which immediately brought my attention back to him.

"We will speak of the physical differences that concern you so greatly, my daughter. On your planet, you have facial bone structure differences and color variations according to the geological and climatic areas which have brought about these adaptations. These racial differences enable you to recognize from which country people come. Even within individual continents, one can identify a variety of nationalities by distinctive facial features. You know immediately their Earthly root origin.

"So you can see it is natural that we too have differences, one planet to another because of our roots and the conditions under which we live. Do know that we are basically the same, albeit with a variety of features, as have all human beings on Earth. Surely this is not too difficult to understand.

"For the sake of man, despite our differences, we have united to be of use to you. It is for the reason stated that those who have seen us or who have recognized our existence have seen differing forms. Is this helpful to you? Remember, there is only one mind," he added gently.

Once more he was interrupted by a dome-head. When he had finished, he turned once more to me.

"To resume. You know, daughter, mankind could easily redress the state of affairs into which they have thrown themselves. You see, mankind is in charge of its destiny if it wishes to, and even now can rebalance all aspects of its future. Mankind must not be allowed to sit down and become complacent. An agitation and stirring up of thought patterns is required. When the agitation settles, the pattern will have changed into a clearer perspective. That is our intention, that is our hope."

I wondered who was to do the stirring and agitating and hoped it would not have to be my role. I had never considered myself as an agitator, rather the opposite.

Osishoo stood up. "I would like you to meet one of our Elders," he said. "I am sorry it is to be through the viewing screen as a recorded message for Earth. You will have no difficulty in understanding the thought that went into the making of it."

The lights dimmed in the room. All that could be heard was a slight hum. I sat quietly, tight with anticipation. Would the speech be through my mind as it had been so far? I felt Andreas touch me on the arm, reassuring me.

The screen came alive, glowing softly. A figure very much like Osishoo appeared, but with eyes of electric blue, quite startling in effect. He began to speak in the same strange swishing sound that Osishoo used. Each word was emphasized and drawn out. The dome-heads stopped what they were doing to watch, and I knew that this was an important person.

"We must begin. We need to begin. We come as the wind. We come as invisible as the wind *(to Earth).* We come many times when you see our movements, but not our form. As we move among you, our activity creates a disturbance of pattern, which makes us known to those who notice. We bring with us many things which settle into your ground unnoticed, but real and existing. What we bring settles and has an effect. The seeds settle also within the form of (*human*) beings, unseen and unnoticed. They pass into the density of matter with ease."

I felt the pressure of Andreas's hand tighten on my arm. What this man was saying sounded like sowing seeds, invisible sowing.

"This is happening in many areas of our choosing," the upright figure said, staring straight ahead. "There is penetration of our essence in such a gentle way that it is unknown to you. We do this to good effect and upon instructions which have been given to us. Many of the worlds about you are also acting on instructions. We have been training for some considerable time as to the best way of carrying out this gentle penetration of our essence.

"Wherever our seed falls, it is taken in by means of absorption to the very core of your beings, having an effect upon you. We are not alone. There are many similar to us who have received instructions, not of an identical nature but with the same purpose in mind. We are all aware of the purpose of the Divine Plan and of the benefits that our action will bring. You will not all be aware immediately, as we have been instructed to be gentle and imperceptible, so as not to cause unnecessary alarm or investigation."

I remembered the phrase "There are more things in heaven and earth" and thought how true that was.

The silver figure raised his arms. "You wonder then why we are advising you now of our actions. We are responding to the many queries that are in the minds of souls like you, those who are ready to accept. You ask, what are these changes and how are they to come about?"

I sat up straight at this. Would we be told now or later? Would I remember if I were to be told now? I already was aware that I was subjected to a procedure of amnesia after some of my visits.

He continued his speech, "Our process of integration requires much more than thought contact. It requires an elaborate and complicated system of exchange through time and space. The exchange is made at certain favorable times in relation to positioning of the universes that surround you. It is an exciting project for us. You might call it an exciting experiment, though we do not consider it to be truly an experiment for we are aware of the outcome. We are confident that the instructions given to us come from those who have a greater knowledge and wisdom.

"We have satellites of our own. Energies are being directed through the satellites from point to point. If you could see these energies, you would call them a grid. Be assured that although we have a certain control and a specific plan, we cannot at any time force ourselves against the will of individuals. We can influence, we can suggest. We can attach thought patterns, but if these are to no effect, we can do nothing."

I leaned over to Andreas and whispered in his ear. "That should be a relief to those who don't like to change at all."

"Shush! Pay attention." Andreas cautioned.

"Do not be alarmed by any slight variations in your behavior or reaction to matter around you. These variations are to be minimal and do not indicate illness or permanent damage, unless you are already ill, which has nothing to do with us. These variations indicate change, which may take some little time to become accustomed to. It is like the visual experiments conducted by your scientists using spectacles which reversed vision, making everything appear upside down. This took very little time for the volunteer to adjust to and quite soon his vision returned to normal even while wearing the special glasses. So you see, in the same way, your physical form will readjust to a perfectly functioning body after any changes we may make within you. Do not be disturbed."

I turned to Osishoo. "Can I ask questions?"

"You may ask *me*, if you like," he replied, rapidly blinking his sharp eyes.

"With our communication here and now, we are using thought transference, aren't we?" I asked. "I just want to get it straight."

"Yes, I think that explains it sufficiently." His eyes flickered.

"Will we on Earth develop telepathic communication as a result of these changes?"

"Yes, this is already developing on Earth and will increase. The minds of men will expand in diverse ways from what has been the normal pattern so far. There is to be an increase both in telepathic communication and sensing and awareness in many areas, such as healing abilities. It is for this we need your help. There needs to be a realization that these gifts are already within each one of you before they can be made manifest in actual activity."

I pressed him further. "Doesn't telepathy mean an invasion of privacy to some people? They wouldn't be keen to have people read their thoughts."

"It is not like that at all," he answered. "As in most communication, it requires at least two people to be receptive. There would be a blocking if one did not desire to receive. There has to be an agreement to this method being used. To use it against another's will is considered a misguided act and would be condemned. If, however, there is an attempt at communication out of loving care, this is acceptable. As in all matters of relating one to another, one should act for the good and not ill intent. Overall, the benefits will outweigh the disadvantages."

"Thank you for the explanation and reassurance," I said, relieved.

His eyes flickered again, and I knew he was pleased. He pointed to the screen, indicating I was to listen again.

The silver figure began transmitting, "There is change all the time. The structure of the body adapts itself to changes in the environment, through evolution, as it has done throughout the ages. However, we have not sufficient time for this to be done as in the past. Cellular and physical changes are taking place more speedily to enable suitable vehicles for souls to continue comfortably within the environment which man has himself brought about.

"Those who pass from this current incarnation will, in many cases, reincarnate with a modified structure of physical being. It will be scarcely noticeable and undetected, but there will be changes just the same."

This must be what was referred to when I was told about the DNA difference during the reading in Washington DC, I thought.

"In part," broke in Osishoo, who had picked up my thought. Do not feel that nothing of life exists outside of your sphere of knowledge. *We* exist even if you cannot touch us or see or experience. We do not wish to see extinction of species any more than you. We bemoan the fate of species on your planet that are becoming extinct and like you. We in our way are trying to preserve that which is in danger from the environment. You are not the only life forms to attempt or be concerned about conservation of the variety that exists. Meaning that we too are concerned. We will do our best but in reality you can best help yourselves.

The Elder on the screen took on a more serious tone and continued:

"There will be changes in molecular structure. It is inevitable. Those that withstand the structural changes within the cells will be best suited to the environment. There will be surprising mutations, any change of cell is after all a mutation. This change will not be by easy evolutionary process. It will take effect in a short span of time, not overnight but in terms of evolution, but a brief span. We are not speaking of many generations, rather fewer.

"Genetic change will not affect mankind alone. All the life forms will be adjusted, mutated, some more than others according to the level of exposure. Do not be alarmed. It is not a process for alarm, it is merely a continuation of life, albeit in a slightly adjusted form. Life will exist, souls, spirits will continue to inhabit an Earthly vehicle. It is therefore as important as before that progress is made in the spiritual striving for perfection. Unity of the whole is as valid as it ever was and ever will be, we ourselves included.

"What matters is that there is a physical carriage for each soul, in order for life experiences to continue. It would be beneficial for man to adopt the attitude of mind that the vehicle they inhabit is not the main concern. Whatever form it takes, it is important to keep that form in good maintenance and not to abuse it. What is of greater significance is the development of mind and soul of man, which is the prime reason for existence in a physical form." The Elder left the screen.

I felt Andreas nudge my arm again, calling my attention. The screen now showed a lot of people resting on the ground. Andreas shifted in his chair and nodded to Osishoo. I knew communication had passed between them but was not given to me. The birdman nodded back in agreement.

"What's going on?" I asked. "What are you saying?"

Osishoo pointed to the screen, which now showed one or two people stepping over and threading their way through all the recumbent bodies on the ground, stirring them with a stick.

Osishoo turned the full power of his piercing eyes on me. "Do you think you can stir your fellow humans to action, to help them to come out of their apathy and change what they do not like about their existence?"

I looked away. So they *do* have me down as an agitator and stirrer. Don't they know that's not my kind of thing at all? Peace at any price, that's me.

They waited together for my response. I had an idea that they would wait all day if need be, if I took that long to answer.

"I can try," I said at last. "That's the best I can do."

Osishoo appeared to beam, if a birdman can beam. "Turn to face me, my daughter, and look into my eyes." Obediently, I did as I was told.

Astonished at the vast depths in those unblinking dark eyes, my whole being was drawn into them. I lost myself in scenes I could see there. What was happening? I stopped resisting and allowed my mind to become absorbed.

Osishoo shook his silver head. "Let us speak of dwellings now. These have to be aligned correctly. Dwellings should be aligned along the correct paths according to advice and instruction from those who can feel the sensations. Everyone will benefit if those with acute senses are accorded due attention. It may not be clear initially that the benefits will be in energy, good health, and protection against those things yet unseen. We are instructing you now so that this knowledge may be recorded and passed to those who will understand."

"Are you speaking of feng shui?" I asked.

"To some degree, yes. But this is but one tiny portion of the instruction to come. You have more to experience. Focus on my eyes."

Again I found myself in a new landscape. This time I stood staring at huge snowcapped mountains on the other side of great pyramids, which appeared small in comparison.

"Waters once flowed off these mountains, providing the necessary moisture for growth." Osishoo's sadness surprised me. I watched in awe as the mountains tumbled. How can one destroy mountains?

Osishoo's strange swishing voice explained, "Deforestation has an impact too. They are mountains that moved in destruction. It may happen again as an inevitable consequence of a sudden momentary halting, which is sufficient to create the alteration. Landscape, waters, all can be altered in an instant. Many will see a change, though there may be areas less affected than others. All will see the consequences, if their eyes are able. Mountains will be where there were none before. Positions will be altered. Do not be fearful."

I found myself drawn more deeply into Osishoo's large eyes and knew I was still being directed by his mind. Black clouds came, darkening the sky until it was difficult to see the land.

His voice explained once more. "The lights will have to be lit if you are to see. It will be time to light the lamps when the darkness descends."

I remembered a poem that had been given to me from my communicators in spirit.

Souls who wander through the night
do so in search of light.
We set lanterns along the way
until they reach the light of day.
You are our lanterns bright and clear.
To us you are held most dear.

He was still speaking. "Earth shaken by a blast of noise. Vibration moves all in its path and which cannot be stopped by human hands. This is a natural consequence of sound force, through a sound that is not in tune. It cannot and will not diminish, for the pattern has been set. It will be a shaking, no more than that. But it is one that will be noticed and one that will cause many to fear and question and to wonder if this is the beginning of something greater. Do not fear. All is in hand to bring about a healing and a change in attitudes of those who will not make their own adjustments."

I was stunned as I sat between Andreas and this great silver figure. "When?" I whispered.

"It would not be in the interests of any to know when. You cannot alter this event. You have no control over this. We are watchful over your souls and are ever mindful of you. You are not forsaken. Those who are around you to assist and guide and comfort will, as always, remain in their duties towards you. Continue in your spiritual growth, and you will be aware of the assistance given you."

I wanted more reassurance than that. "Is this why I and others like me are urged to make it known that there is a continuation of life no matter what happens?"

"Try to continue with the healing of the soul. We come not

from your world, not from your plane of existence. We come to assist, to soothe the pain that exists on your world. We come to add balm to sore and troubled spots." He blinked his dark eyes rapidly as he finished speaking.

I knew that many people would not be encouraged by that at all, especially if they had no idea of the existence of these other worlds.

"It seems to me that you have spoken of changes in our physical form, of land changes and unsettling political events and climatic changes, quite apart from a need to grow in spiritual understanding," I said. "It is all rather a lot to take in and get to grips with. I do not think anyone will be able to accept this if I say anything. Especially if they have not personally experienced it as I have. They might even put me away for psychiatric therapy."

Osishoo was sympathetic. "Daughter, you are not alone in receiving this information. Many others beside you are going through the same experiences. Therefore you will not be a lone voice. The main purpose of passing on this advance notice is to encourage the raising of vibrations and spiritual understanding. When this occurs, whatever happens physically is not seen to be so important, for one is able to meet any challenge that is offered. What is more, many negative events can be avoided or lessened in its impact. Negativity attracts negativity, and a positive approach encourages positive experiences."

Still held in the mirror of his eyes, I suddenly saw birds, lots of birds flying in an orderly sweep round, coming in to land. They then rose up in a body, wings all flapping together in unison. Very close to us, I could see the flapping of their wings all around me. They did not stay near the ground but flew higher and higher until they disappeared from view.

Osishoo's voice interrupted my thoughts once more. "The birds have gone to their feeding grounds, where they will be nourished. They will grow fat and be strengthened in knowledge and abilities. They will return in greater numbers after the winter of your time. Their numbers will multiply. They will drop the seeds that they have been fed with in their homeland. This is inevitable, and there need be no fear that this will not happen. They will remain away *(from Earth?)* until the cold has passed, when they will be given the signal for the time of new life. They will return. It is for each to interpret this message as they will."

Just as the Bible is interpreted in many ways, I thought. That will cause a kerfuffle all right, that is, if anybody takes any notice in the first place of that symbolic message. I remembered that Osishoo himself was a birdman.

He continued, "We too are coming in greater numbers, but will not wait for the warming of the spring. We are those who come in time of need to replace those who have returned home. We will be found in large numbers and groups in human form throughout your globe. We will be spread so that we are unnoticed, but ever effective. We are to assist whenever there is a call. Do not feel that assistance comes only from the spirit world. Already on your Earth are others from areas yet unknown to you in your current life. We are already present and directed by those who have a larger viewpoint, those who are in a position to overview the entire situation. These ones send their directions to us."

I thought again of the Looking Glass equipment and wondered just how far ahead they could see. I realized the greater part of this message was symbolic in meaning, for surely actual birds were not intended? As he said, it was for each to interpret. I did not ask for an explanation, for I knew I would not be given one this time.

"Thank you for your understanding and participation in the mind work," he said. With a whoosh, I was released from his mind and sitting comfortably with Andreas, watching Osishoo blinking his enormous eyes. I felt his smile rather than saw it when Andreas took my arm and guided me out of the door once more.

I began to feel so tired I didn't think I could stay standing. "I feel weary," I told Andreas, yawning.

"It is time you rested. All this is quite a strain on the mind if you are not used to it. We may have to return you if you are not sufficiently refreshed after a few hours. I daresay something can be arranged at another time, though we may have to wait quite a while for the life-support system to be in a favorable position once more." Andreas guided me into my room. It was time to sleep.

I woke and forgot where I was. What day was it? Gradually, it all came back. Home seemed to be so distant. I was homesick and wished to go back to what one could call normality. I longed to talk naturally to people again about ordinary day-to-day things. Would I ever be able to do that again? It was all too much.

I investigated the panel of supplies when loud bells began ringing insistently. Something was happening. It was an alarm of some kind. Andreas arrived. I could tell from his expression that something was up, though he was as calm as usual and glowing even more brightly.

"What's going on?" I asked anxiously.

"There is a need to shift the positioning," he answered. "The decision to allow you to stay or not does not rest with me now. We must leave while we have the correct 'gateway' coordinates. Come on, hurry."

"Why must they move the system? Surely it can't be seen by anyone?" I objected to being rushed off like a parcel.

"Man has increased technologically and is discovering much. However, spiritual responsibility and wisdom do not always go hand in hand with this knowledge. A space probe from Earth, with its many ways of scanning, is approaching, and we do not wish the system to be viewed in a specialized camera range. Therefore, the Controllers must change their location," he explained as he pushed me through the door.

"How am I going to get back home?" I said, puffing as I hurried after him.

"Leave that to us," he said as we quickly entered the room where we had arrived. The scene that met my eyes was one of great activity. The dome-heads were busy at their consoles and took no notice of us at all. It crossed my mind that they must be used to visitors from different planets and took it as normal. Osishoo arrived, creating a stir. He towered above the dome-heads. It was clear he held an important command position.

"We will meet again, daughter," he said. "One day I will teach you our language, but now you must leave while you can." The great eyes blinked at me, giving me a glimpse of profound knowledge behind them. Once more I submerged my own identity in them and lost all awareness.

As if from a vast distance, I heard him say, "Sit here." An arm guided me to a chair where my head became fuzzier and fuzzier. Like being anesthetized, I thought as my head began to swim round and round. I left and woke up in my own bed at home. Had it all really happened?

It was around this period that I had many messages relating to the presence of interplanetary beings on and around our planet. It is also clear from these messages that their only intention is to assist in our evolution and to stop us from making a mess of things. If they had wanted to do us harm, they have had plenty of opportunity and have not done so over the past thousands, perhaps millions, of years. The messages are still coming. I give you some of their words here:

"Osishoo and his kind are going to inhabit the Earth alongside humans—when humans have raised their vibrations enough. You will learn to live in harmony and peace with other nations. If you can't do that, how can you do it with intergalactic intelligence? Your role is to prepare Earth people to be comfortable with the new races, not to fear them. You will benefit by them being here. No difference in soul content, just physical form. You are preparing the way."

In recent years till the present day the preparation has taken another turn. I have begun to speak their language and by that I mean many of their cosmic languages. It began during channelling for groups or to individuals. They explained that although it could not be interpreted literally the vibration of the sounds produced enabled healing, either physically or emotionally. Those present said they felt it and were helped. I am now able to understand the gist of the meaning if not the actual words. I am able to interpret. For myself it is a huge pleasure and I love doing it. Many others are also engaged in this and call it '*Light language*'. Personally I call it '*Cosmic language' or 'Star Language'*..

I believe rightly or wrongly that those who speak this strange language are to be the interpreters when our cosmic cousins make themselves physically known on our planet. As they said to me, not everybody is telepathic. Make of that what you will.

I have since met many who can write in Space language and understand it.

Chapter 23

Other Species

We are not meant to be apart.
Unite with us with loving heart.
Friends of the Earth are we,
who wish to share the Earth with thee.
Join with us in our joy and use the methods
we employ
To unite us all as one great Soul,
To bring us back into the Whole.
We are all of one Divine Creation,
All worlds and every nation.

Birdman Osishoo

It was not long before I was shown that other beings exist on our Earth and that we humans are not the only intelligent species here. There are others besides us, who have as much right to a peaceful Earth as we do.

I was walking with a group on Easter Island in 2006, when I was telepathically told to look over a cliff and I would receive a surprise. This I did and saw to my delight a cluster of different kinds of nonhuman beings. They were at the foot of the cliff collecting specimens. Some of them waved to me when they realized I had seen them. My spirit communication told me that they had been doing this long before we humans were on the

Earth and were still regular visitors for research purposes.

Pixies and Elves

I go into meditation. The walk is through trees, dried crackly leaves, and brittle twigs. It is winter. Everything cracks, and the air is dry and thin. I am walking inside a winter forest. Because it is winter, I can see through the trees. I come to a downward slope off the path. I slither down the incline into a great pile of leaves at the bottom. I can't stop the slide. It is like a funnel, for I slide into the spout of the funnel and tumble out the other end where it is warm and cozy—I am underground. There are people here. Not normal people, for they remind me of elves and pixies. I do not understand this at all.

"Although we are human looking, we are another species, a completely different species never to be mingled or matched genetically. We will always remain separate in form. We belong to this Earth and are citizens of the Earth, every bit as much as you. Therefore, we too have a right to feel and to say what we feel about the doings on the surface that damage so much."

The theme continued with another journey.

Fairies Release Joy

The steps have a metal bar across, edging it to stop the wear on the tread. It is very austere and derelict here. I cannot see the bottom, although the steps are not steep. I keep going down, holding on to an unpainted wooden rail at the side. Everything has been neglected, though I feel it is still used, otherwise they would not have the rail or the metal strip across the steps. Some care is being taken because people do use it. I can see the bottom now. The floor is of broken tiles. I get the feeling of being in a building that has not been used for a while and has been allowed to disintegrate. I see offices such as one would get in an old warehouse with the corridor running between them, windowed offices. There are lots of windows running along the entire length of the corridor. I come to a door, a cheap office door. No luxury here. I push the door open. I step inside. It is quite light, plenty of space, an empty office. One almost expects there to be squatters because the building itself is sound but is just unused and left to rot.

I look around me and see desks. There is one over to the right, piled high with an odd jumble of papers and files, all piled up in a heap. No order attached to it. I walk over to it and fiddle around, trying to pull something substantial from the pile. There is a thick bulky file underneath all the heavy papers. It is in black. I open it. This is bizarre. As I open it I see dancing figures like in a fairy story, only these figures are alive and dancing across the pages. I do not know what this is trying to tell me, but it is delightful. Such joy is there in opening this book again. The spirits have been in the book all this time waiting for someone to come along and release them. They are leaping off the pages and dancing about the room. Little fairy figures dancing about in absolute delight. Oh, they are beautiful. I still do not know what this means.

"The fairies of thought, the fairies of ideas, the fairies of creation, the thoughts that have gone into these pages, have been released from the dust of old time and are free now to fly away themselves wherever they feel fit to go."

They scatter around the room, stirring the dust, sweeping the dust, and touching everything with magical light, transforming the dusty office into something bright and shining. I still do not know how this relates to me and to anything I must do.

I suddenly see a tall shining form, standing in the corner, watching all this. It is a beautiful spirit figure watching with a smile. I go up to him. The fairies are still dancing around and enjoying themselves. I ask him what this means for me.

"Release the thoughts that have been buried, not only in you but in others. Release the trapped joy that is in everyone's life story. Release the gladness that is there waiting, so that renewed life may come. It is not that you bring them gladness, for they already have it, but as in so many, it is trapped. They need someone from outside themselves to help them open their hearts and their memories that have lain dormant in the dust of their past. Allow this renewed joy and creation to flourish in the present time. Help them see what lies within. This goes for you too, for you are not exempt from burying what you prefer to forget or burying the goodness that lies inside you from your past."

The little fairy figures have grouped together and formed a ring. They are holding hands and dancing around clockwise, creating a continuous circle. They move faster and faster until they form just one spinning band of colored light. They create a vortex which, as they move faster and faster, moves upwards like a column of light, with the fairies at the top of the column as it pushes upwards. The column reaches up and goes through the ceiling out into the sky. It goes higher and higher until the top of it goes out of my sight. It is a beautiful pillar of light from the center of the room, created by fairy figures. As I look at the column, the glowing figure in the corner moves towards me, takes me by the hand, and walks me forward so that we are both standing in the column and are encircled by the column of light. We both disappear, and the room is left empty. Although I am not there, I can see the empty room. And that is all. I am back.

An Inner Journey: Intelligent Species Survive in the Earth

It becomes easier as I go further down, and at the bottom is shingle. I walk forward, shifting on the shingle as I go. I follow my nose and turn off, looking for some means to get in. There is a crack, an opening between two boulders. This is it. I climb through. There is no difficulty, but I must climb through. This is physical.

I feel the presence of others here. I cannot see anybody, but I know I am not alone.

I shout out loud, "Show me what I need to see." I feel the others are from another planet. They are not of this Earth. I can just see them now, shadowy. There one minute and not the next. I have to be quick to see them. It is like trying to see a shadow that is moving. If I am to communicate with them, they must show themselves more clearly or stay still. They are inquisitive.

Soon they are all over me, little ones pulling, investigating, curious, and not harming me at all. I don't feel frightened of them. They are just testing me in a sense, feeling the vibrations of me and deciding if I am all right through a sense of touch. They use touch and vibration to decide. I realize that they cannot see. They are blind. They sense me in the same way that I sensed them. They cannot see but can sense, which is why they're feeling me much as a blind person would do. They operate through the mind.

"We will teach you how to survive in the earth. We will teach you not with words but with knowledge and ideas, a knowing so that when the occasion arises, you will simply know what to do."

"Wouldn't it help me to know in advance?"

"No, it would not help you, for you would tell your mind and your subconscious that it is impossible. But when the occasion arises, you will know, and it will be possible. It does not help to have advance knowledge of this. Information will be there when you need it. We did not always exist inside the earth. There was a time when we lived on the surface also."

I am confused now. I cannot think clearly. Something is going on. Maybe input is taking place now. I cannot think of anything else.

Another Species—Citizens of the Earth

During a later channeling to a group of people, I was shown clusters of white, very thin long people who were clearly not our usual human being. *(Tall Whites?)* They were coming out of the mountains, and I felt they had been living there inside for a long time.

"We have been on Earth for many generations, and the time is coming when we will come out and be with the people openly."

The evening was set up with the intention of calling in the space visitors. The following is the result.

"We are highly amused when you ask to call in extra-terrestrials, meaning not of the Earth. You yourselves did not originate on your current home planet. Likewise, we are all of the Earth, even those communicating with you now. For we have been current in the Earth for many years and have earned the right to say that we are citizens of the Earth. Generally, we regard ourselves as citizens of the cosmos.

"But now we are speaking from a base, not on your soil. We are speaking from a command post. In case any of you ask where we come from, for that is in your minds, we tell you that this force is a combination of species. That is to say that we are many from a variety of planetary systems. We have come together under a Command to see the Earth through its evolution and to monitor the progress of its peoples, to ensure that there is no total annihilation. If we did not monitor, if we did not interfere, then man would have already been extinguished by his own hand. So, you see we are not invaders, we do not wish to take you over. We do wish that you continue in your evolutionary program. You might say that you are our children. Were it not for these varieties that now patrol the periphery of your planet, were it not for these species, you would not exist."

New entity enters: "We speak now from an area much closer to your planet. We too have been with the planet Earth since the beginnings of *Homo sapiens*. We are very similar to you in form, not all identical. Some are extremely tall, some extremely short. We get on well with each other. We can travel dimensionally, spatially, mentally, and telepathically. You might say we are here, there, and everywhere, though it is not quite as disordered as that. We operate under a control, a command known as a Confederation. We are regulated by celestial beings. We are regulated by and work in harmony with those you regard as your Ascended Masters, those who have had incarnations on your planet Earth as known beings in past times. They are advanced souls whose endeavor is to bring humanity into a new state, a new race. It is our endeavor collectively with the Brotherhood and a variety of non-earthly beings, intelligent species, to ensure a smooth changeover.

"This program has been in place for thousands of years. We are attempting this gradually rather than dramatically. It entails genetic manipulation, it entails introduction of new ideas, consciousness, and awareness through a variety of means, such as subconsciously. There is a whole range of methods used to speed the growth of the human soul and human understanding. We need to do this carefully and gently, though at times when the consciousness of an individual is close to the subconscious so that there is very little difference between them, then there is an awareness of what we do at times.

"Sometimes the adjustments we need to make physically are done in your subconscious state, an amnesiac situation. Those who find it difficult to be hypnotized or to go into a deeper state are aware of what is happening to them. This may arouse a fear in them. Many of you have had adjustments made to you and, after the events, have had this amnesiac process so that you do not remember.

Q. "After these adjustments do we have headaches?"

"Much as in your normal medication, the reactions vary. For some, there are headaches, which may last for a time. It is regrettable, but it is of benefit once the headaches die down, once things are in place. It is similar in some way to having a pin put through a broken limb, which is uncomfortable until one becomes used to it. Then the limb becomes mended. It is not a good analogy but will help you understand. We try to do this gently and by slow degrees. Sometimes the headaches are produced because we have reactivated a gene, a part of DNA in your system. This action after a long atrophy can cause a discomfort until it has integrated well. Some of you may feel odd pains, unexplainable pains in a variety of places. There may be mental confusion at times while the brain impulses readjust themselves to the new action takes place."

Q. "Does it cause blood pressure?"

"It can do. We are not saying that all causes of blood pressure are because of our interaction. If you have blood pressure, we suggest that you check this out with your doctor and reassure yourself from where it is coming. To give you a blanket answer would be detrimental to many who have blood pressure. We do not ask you to ignore it."

"Some of you will want to sleep more than usual. It will be sleepiness rather than a physical tiredness."

Q. "Do you do it with everybody?"

"We try not to be judgmental. There are some individuals where we would be wasting our time. There are individuals who would prefer that we leave them in the state that they are in. It is their soul's choice. We honor this right. So the answer to that is no, we do not do it with everybody.

"We focus on those who have in their soul aspiration to be of service, to assist others, who have qualities that would be of benefit to their fellow man. In the same way, it would be ridiculous to teach a difficult musical instrument to one who had no interest in music. Eventually all will arrive. You will find a disparity between individuals. We work with the Ascended Masters. We sit in council with them.

"We decide where placement of our life-support systems is best suited. We invite many souls from Earth to visit us so that they may have in their memories knowledge of what we try to do. We work closely with the planet Earth and many individuals who are working there. We do not work in isolation. It is a combination of forces. We attempt to influence the consciousness of those in authority. Sometimes we are successful, and sometimes we are not. You have questions. I can feel them." *(Heartbeat heard on tape)*

Q. "You know the Ascended Masters? This is a query that has just come up. What I have learnt so far is that Serapis Bey comes in a golden ray. Can you shed any light on that?"

"Yes. Serapis Bey is indeed working with us, as are the others."

More recently, in October 2009, I had a conversation with Serapis Bey, who did not disclose who he was until the end. I was asking for more tangible evidence of the presence of space beings here on Earth. I would not have spoken to him in the way that I did if I had known who he was.

Here is just some of what was said during a meditation: The scene around me is changing. I am in another land, another dimension, another time. It is very real. Nobody is surprised to see me, though I have just arrived. They must be used to this. I am just another arrival, and there are many like me.

I seem to know where to go. I do not need to be led. I walk along a definite path. I am quite determined and know exactly where I am going. I go to a building, not as we have, but is circular with a spire on top of a dome. I walk into this. I am to meet with a group of people here. I have been invited but am there by choice. *I don't know who I am.*

I am shown into a room. There are mostly men sitting at various workstations. I march up to one of them, who is very tall. He is an extra-terrestrial, space brother.

"We are all space brothers, a space family unit, a space command. You have been asking to meet with us."

I say forcefully and impatiently, "I meant I wished to meet space brothers physically here on Earth, not up here in another time. What I need is to be adjusted to those here on Earth, even if they come in human form. I need to be linked to them so that we have something in common between us when the work begins. It is important, for how else can I help the unaware ones if I have not had the experience first?"

"You are having the experience."

"You misunderstand me. I mean on Earth, physically on Earth so that I may be comfortable with them myself, so that others can be made comfortable. You can understand that surely."

They do not seem to understand the needs of a human being.

"I am here as a human being. I wish to interact fully with the space brothers on Earth. It is all very well meeting like this, but it does not prepare the human being that I am *(have become)* for the work I must do. (*said firmly*) This is a request."

"It is noted."

"I would hope it is more than noted because I need some action here. I need some answers. I need one of your kind to help us understand the languages that are being given to myself and others here. (*I am at this time speaking in several off-world languages*.) We need a teacher for this in the same way as you would have a teacher in the classroom when learning another language. We need an intermediary. If we are to become intermediaries ourselves, we must have more assistance from you here."

"We have noted."

I am getting frustrated now. "Noting is one thing, doing is another," I said. "Maybe I am being presumptuous here, but I need something more, much more."

One of them stands up and waves his finger at me. A wave, a current of energy envelops me all over so I am changed. I am changed now forever.

"You are not human, are you?" I ask.

"I was once."

"That's interesting. Who were you?"

"I am now, Serapis Bey."

"Ah! So, Serapis Bey, you were human, and now?"

"I am a space friend."

All of this was conducted on an equal basis, with neither being more authoritative than the other.

Chapter 24

The Program Is in Hand

The chaotic free electron changes to an orderly predictable pattern when watched by a human observer. The Human Mind can control the atom. THOUGHTS ARE THINGS.

The Universe needs the minds of men as an observer for nothing is said to exist until it is observed. Therefore when you visualise something within your mind, because you have observed it, it from then on exists. As you observe your thoughts will be entering your mind in relation to it. These thoughts too are changing matter (atoms).

I was again to be reminded that all was arranged, and I should not be concerned. The prompt came in the usual way with a meditation.

I walk down a ramp similar to airport ramps for luggage trolleys, zigzagging down, floor by floor such as at Terminal 1 at Heathrow. I am not pushing a trolley, though I feel I ought to be, as the connection in my mind with airports is so strong. I get to the bottom, and yes, I see I have got a trolley now. It is there with luggage on it. It is heavy. I push it forward.

This *is* an airport. The doors open to the right, I push the trolley through. I've no idea where I am going. I appear to have arrived and am not departing. I push the trolley out to where all the taxis and buses are waiting. It is a busy scene.

A big car pulls up, and it is for me. It's an official car, one of the stretch Limo jobs. My goodness! The luggage is loaded in the back, and I am invited to get in. I sit in front and get whisked away. I don't know where to or where I am. There are tall buildings, lots of very busy traffic. I suddenly realize somebody is sitting in the car with me but at the back, quietly observing. Who is it? He puts out a hand and touches me on the shoulder, as if to reassure me. We drive out into the country. The car pulls up into a lay-by *(pull off viewing point)* overlooking the land. Beyond the land is the sea. I get out, and the man gets out too. We stand in silence looking over a long, distant view. There is a haze over the horizon which stretches as far as the eye can see.

The man again puts his hand on my shoulder and says, "Yes, that is the land you have to encompass and cover with words and actions."

I think, "Well, I don't even know where I am, let alone have a program."

"Do you think it has not all been arranged? Else, how could the transport have been waiting for you if we did not have a program in mind? We have organized it. We will ensure that you are at the correct place at the correct time to do your work. All you need do is acquire the knowledge and ability to do it. You may leave the rest to us. So, while you are waiting for this, learn, absorb, and put into practice so that when we call you are ready."

I feel quite comfortable with that. It takes the pressure off me, not having to worry about organizing where to go and who to see. I feel much better about that. All I am left with is the work. I get back in the car, and so does he. There is a child there now, sitting between us. We are all in the back seat now. The child is a little girl of about five or six. How she came there or why, I do not know. I ask.

He replies, "The child is wise and a protection."

I do not understand that. The cold is coming over me now. Somebody is coming into me. The cold is quite intense. It is a Native American, a strong male. He is with me now, a man of few words. He should realize I need the words or to hear his thoughts. They must be voiced. I invite him to voice his thoughts.

"Work, and you will be rewarded. Stay idle, and you will receive nothing."

Oh, it is so cold!

I often dwell on why they give me such a long-protracted journey that seems not to be important. As usual, my thoughts bring an answer.

"A journey is a necessary technique to take your mind away from the conscious state and to connect with your subconscious mind. This will always, at all times give you what is correct and true without interference from logical everyday consciousness."

I realise now that in order to go into a deep subconscious state I need whatever preparation is suitable to take my mind away from everyday matters, which creep in otherwise. The journey given is so intriguing that the mind wants to stay with it. It is a bit like having a dream that you do not want to come out of because is it so interesting.

Chapter 25

Mass Soul Rescue

Life is too short to wake up with regrets. So love the people who treat you right. Forget about those who don't. Believe everything happens for a reason. If you get a second chance, grab it with both hands. If it changes your life, let it. Nobody said life would be easy, they just promised it would be worth it.

It was not long after that experience that I was called on again, this time for souls who had departed but who had so much trauma and negative experiences during their lives that they were stuck in a self-imposed hell.
It began with a meditation.

Frightened Souls: On My Journey
I have a blue cloud. I step into the cloud, and it carries me up. I'm inside it rather like a special conveyance designed for the purpose. I know I have arrived at wherever I am going because a little flight of steps is thrust into the cloud, rather as one would put steps up to an aeroplane when it lands. (*I think they have a sense of humor.*) I go up out of the cloud and stand there for a moment, not knowing what I should do.

I ask, "Please show me where to go."

A hand reaches out and takes my hand. I follow as it pulls

me along. It is as if I am walking on nothing. I am drawn along with the hand until I almost run smack-bang into a fence. It is strange because they are real boards, the sort you would get in a hoarding. I feel around for some sort of opening because I cannot go through it. It is better if I go in the correct way, and so I feel along the edge until I feel a catch. I lift the catch, and it slides the hoarding to one side. I step into whatever is on the other side. I am on rough stone, the sort you could stumble on if you do not position your feet carefully. Rough ground.

I know instinctively that in this place there are souls who need some assistance. They are living in a way that is full of despair. The hopelessness pervades the air. No hope and nobody to visit them because who wants to go to an area like this? Nobody! I have been brought here, so I must find these souls because they are afraid and are hiding.

They know I am here. I walk carefully, picking my feet over the stones, the rocks, and rubble. Rubble is the right word for this, and I look into dark corners and I know that people, fearful souls are hiding. I find myself a piece of ground and smooth it out. I sit there as comfortably as I am able, and I send my thoughts to them to come out, that there is nothing to be afraid of.

I look all around, and I say out loud, "COME OUT SO THAT I CAN SEE YOU, SO THAT WE CAN TALK."

A little time passes. I do not move, but before long, they come. They come from all around me out of the darkness. I am surprised because there are children, there are old people, there are young people; there is every imaginable age and type of person. They are all in despair, afraid of the world and fearful for themselves. They come out a little hesitantly. I can see their minds are enquiring as to why and who is this one that has come from somewhere else other than their own chosen dwelling place.

I tell them to sit down. They do. I notice my clothes are blue and smooth and are reflecting a glow like a neon. They are lit up by the glow so that I can see their faces. I tell them that they can leave this place and follow me when I leave if they will hold each other's hands. I will hold the hand of the first one. When I leave, if they will follow forming a chain I can show them the way out.

But they are frightened because they want to know what is on the other side of the hoarding. I tell them I do not know for them all, but it is better than where they have been and better than where they are now. It cannot be worse, can it? They think about this. Some of them are not sure whether it is better to stay where they know what is. I hear them think, *"Better the devil we know."* I ignore this and tell them to hold hands and join hands with each other for strength, and a little sheepishly, they do.

I stand up and walk around the circle. It is a triple circle, and I walk around, passing my hand over the heads as I walk. From my hand, there is a stream of blue light. I continue walking in a spiral as I continue round and round. It takes a little time to pass my hand over them all. Soon I have completed all the circles and there is a blue spiral of light over them. I come back through into the center, and I tell them they will be protected by the blue light. They can choose to believe or not, it is their choice, but if they desire to leave, they may do so.

I stand up and take the hand of the nearest one and walk towards my sliding partition, my hoarding door, and those who decide to come join hands and follow as a chain. I have a little child first. I go through the door while they follow me in a little procession. I walk along till I reach my cloud. It is waiting there, rather like a lift. Here, they are terrified and pull back, but I tell them nothing can hurt them. I show them this by walking into the cloud. They follow. As they go, I wonder if there is room for all those linked up. But there is room, and the cloud gets bigger and bigger as they all crowd in.

I ask what is going to happen to them now. I look around and see their faces have hope and expectancy in them for the first time. I feel that they at least have left the area of despair, and when it is obvious there are no more souls coming, the cloud moves upwards; it does not go back down. It moves up gently and softly. We can't see where we are going because we are enclosed in the cotton-wool blue cloud. We also are all in blue, and they are tightly clutching one another's hands, and the little one is still firmly clutching mine.

Then it stops and another pair of steps appears. I say to them, this is where you get out. Because they now have hope, they go up the steps one by one; I do not go with them. I do not know what happens to them, but I know it is better than where they have been. The little one, the last one, is fearful, but hands reach down into the cloud. He takes the hands and goes up the steps to them. As they go, the blue light leaves my clothes, and I am a normal, ordinary everyday color. I am back home again, knowing I must get on with my normal life. I thank God that I do not have any fear in my life.

Chapter 26

Footprints Over the Globe

I Receive Encouragement

Both Raman and dear Dr. Po are with me. They turn around and point to show me something. I look but I cannot see. After a while I see a bowl, like a sunken bath in the ground. I go over to it. It is full of a blue steamy something. All I can see is blue misty stuff rising from it. I am reminded of a chemical experiment when liquid produces a vapor. It is a large bowl. I put my hand into the mist to see how it feels. My hand becomes a little wet. My friends come closer and stand around the rim of the bowl and look into it as if trying to see something. I do likewise. If they think they can see something, then so might I.

I ask them to show me; I need to know. I stare into the swirling vapor. Then it clears, and I see a country, viewed from a long way up. It is the coastline of an entire country, as if I am seeing it from space. I try to see what country it is and realize it is moving. It is the entire planet underneath the vapor and is slowly spinning. Many countries, there are the two Americas, North and South, Australia, Japan, China, and so on. It is the globe. I want to know why I am being shown this. As I look, I see footprints, outlined on the surface of the globe as if somebody is walking over it and leaving their mark behind. It is in a steady straight line. Large footprints—they are my footprints as I walk over the

Earth and leave my print behind.

I say to them, this is all very nice, but how is this going to happen? They look at each other then they look at me and shake their heads. This does not help me at all. I repeat, how is this going to happen? They put their hands out towards me and take mine. They hold both my hands so that all our hands are joined. They pull me close, still holding my hands, which are now buried in theirs. I get the message that we are all involved in this and it will be done. We all work together to see that it does. I am the physical counterpart that can do what they cannot. I am the physical earthly representative. They stay at headquarters and send out their messages to me, while I am the one that must deliver.

I ask them, please give me the ability to relay what they have to say accurately with conviction and no hesitation, but also with clear words that flow correctly and smoothly so that it holds attention throughout with what they have to say. I ask that this begin immediately.

They have now drawn me around to the other side of the circle where there is a table and chair. I'm to sit at this. There is a book and pens. They have put a pen in my hand, the wrong hand. I change it over to my left hand, as I am left-handed. They take it out and put it back in my right hand. I am not clear what this means as I do not write with my right hand. They have put a pen in the other hand now so that I have a pen in both hands. They tell me to write. I begin to write with my left and they shake their heads and say,

"No, both hands."

I try to write with both hands, but do not know quite how I am to do this. My right hand is writing back from the right side of the paper and meets with the left hand. It does not make sense, but I clearly have to try. Perhaps it is using both sides of the brain. At this thought they nod.

"Both sides of the brain. Bring intellect into this, as well as your intuition. Apply your mind in all its facets."

They lift me up and walk me further along, further away from the bowl. As a little group, we go down some steps. They are behind me, making sure I do not turn around and go back. We go quite a long way down. I cannot see where we are going. I begin to see little lights in the darkness and realize with a shock that there are eyes peering out of the dark at me, at all of us. I wonder why I cannot see the faces.

"You would not want to see the faces. We have hidden them from you for your protection."

I am confused by that but will accept what he says. We go on down. The faces that I am not to see are behind us now. We come through an opening at the bottom into brilliant sunshine. Glorious light! Everything is brilliant. It is difficult to adjust the eyes. I take a deep breath, glad to be out in the fresh air. It is a glorious, wonderful feeling.

Dr.Po speaks, "When you have gone through the darkness and have passed all the disturbed souls successfully, then you will come out into the light, where you will be happy and glad to exist. You will remain with us as we will remain with you."

This moves me for there is such sincerity, kindness, and gentleness in his voice. I'm deeply touched by it. I have so many good friends surrounding me, though I know they are not all here.

I stand before him, tears running down my face. I do not know why I am crying. He turns me round and pushes me gently back into the hands of my friends. They comfort me. I feel so very, very cold now and must come out of this, for the cold is too much.

I am reminded of the preparation that Raman gave me when I froze so that I could reach higher dimensions. Had I been there?

I continued to meditate and began to realise that something was changing. Whatever query I had going round and round in my head my spirit helpers seemed to link to it and gave me answers even without asking. I had been wondering who they really were and why were they putting so much effort into teaching me. I suspected it was simply to give me more work at putting it all in a book to share with the world. I sighed.

Celestial Sons

It was in 1992 that a new entity made himself known.

"My name is Andron," he opened with. "I wish to report on various events that are happening in your world. This is a major topic of conversation for us. We discuss at great length what is to be done with your world. We have been doing this for hundreds of years. We have been plotting and planning, making arrangements so that the best solution can be arrived at. All the while we need to contend with the minds of men, which seem to be forever changing.

One of our contingences, which we are and have been executing for quite some time now is an influx of souls who have the creative source at heart. The influx of these souls come as human beings, for how else could they survive on your planet? They have been entering for quite some considerable time. Some have the memory, and others arrive at this understanding later, sometimes after much hardship.

"However the way has now become easier as time goes on simply because there is a growing awareness among these souls of who they are and what their purpose is. They are able to assist newcomers who are coming in waves. The reason for this is so that there are generations after generations of these evolved souls who know of the plan and who have skills beyond the normal range. They have memories of abilities that they are now able to utilise. There are many degrees of densities and many areas in the cosmos from which they are sent.

"We wish to keep this on a light basis to give you a general idea what our plan is and why. When we come into incarnation from other planets, we come with our soul memories and our genetic background. You are going to say, but genes are from father to son, mother to daughter. We say that the soul historical background is also held within your coding. We are able to activate this coding into fullness.

It would be good if your minds were awakened to your earlier times for you would be assisted greatly. Even during your incarnations on other planets there is the process of learning by experience. No one soul can escape this learning process. I have had to undergo this course that had been set for me. The mere fact that I am able to communicate with you is merely one of my abilities. If I were I to incarnate on your planet I would find much difficulty in relating to you. Maybe one day I will need to do this.

"This brings me to the next point. Many souls from other planets may need to incarnate on yours. That being so we need to have the planet in as good a condition as possible, for our sake. You realise that already your planet is in a critical condition. Therefore those of us who are not yet of your Earth have joined together with a group that some call the Celestial Ones, some call The White Brotherhood and a whole variety of other names that have been applied to this group. Many of you have long since needed a title, something to refer and relate to. We say that these ones are Masters, are the Celestial Sons appointed to take care of your planet and the souls that incarnate there. They work always for the Divine Source from which they came. They have invited us to assist them in the knowledge that we will also benefit.

"Many of you have been appointed and trained to receive from the Celestial Ones and ourselves. Because of the variety of minds and concepts of reception from the spirit world, a whole host of titles has been given to us. Do not be confused by this but know that they are all one and the same grouping, acting for the benefit of mankind and the planet Earth. A whole variety of names are now going through your mind, are they not? Some of them you may have come across in your readings and possibly in your own experiences. I can feel your mind racing.

"The time is already here for we have arrived and will continue to do so. Slightly adapted to meet conditions which are changing upon your planet. We will assist those who have not yet been adapted. One might say that our actions will produce a much stronger race of humanity. There is to be over the total globe instant knowledge of healing abilities and the value of communication with the Earth and all that is on it and within it. The knowledge is born with our coming. There is no need for trepidation for we are as you. We simply have a different background, but all come from the same source. Some of you may have come across and recognise these new entries. How may you know them? You will recognise in them qualities of warmth, happiness, a joyousness of spirit. Those of you who can feel the vibrations of others will sense through the energy field the difference from those who are depressed and who do not act according to spiritual laws. Have you not felt when you pass anyone in the street, that at times you feel a strange warmth of energy, even as you pass, and others with a negative energy that you wish to be distanced from? Do you not recognise a sunny soul when you see one? Are others drawn to this sunny soul even when they do not understand why?

"We tell you that the incomers have to go through the process of understanding humanity. That being so, we need also to have incarnation after incarnation in a variety of ways. We said earlier that we have been coming for hundreds of years, indeed thousands in some cases. We bring this to your attention now, for we are coming in greater numbers. There is a need, and the time is approaching when you will need us. We speak to all who may listen and for them to understand. Many of us have endured hardship on your planet, specifically so that we may understand fully the whole range of emotions and trials that humans have had to undergo from their early beginnings. So that we may be compassionate to all of you we too need to undergo these trials, so that we may understand what is required of us. We need to understand your physical makeup, your emotional bodies and your mental bodies. We do not enter lightly for we are now you and you are us.

"How many of you here have come from my place? We came many years ago and settled on a fair land alongside the Celestial Sons, in companionship with them. We began to learn; we began to feel and understand the planet itself. Before that was possible we had to survey the planet, in much the same way that your scientists are now surveying Mars and the other planets in your solar system. We surveyed it."

Chapter 27

Tuaregs—Guardians of the Way

www.shutterstock.com · 1183082299

From the very beginning of my journeys during meditation, I have had three very imposing desert men who came on camels. I was told they were Tuaregs, nomads and wise men of the desert. They do not come often, but when they do, it's always of great significance. My first encounter is depicted in chapter 6, "Past and Future Lives." Through the years, these wonderful men have brought children to me and told me to follow their progress as they are the special ones. They have made sure I meet in the physical these children. I do my best to keep up. I always feel it is an honor to be able to be with these great men. Some of my encounters with them do not fit into this book but all have been valuable to the journey. The following scenes are best interpreted symbolically.

1. Tuaregs—Thinking in the Desert

I've a picture now of—I think it is me—but I'm not on my own. I am standing. I am back in the desert and brushing the sand from my clothes, as if I have just got up from sitting in the sand, resting. I prepare to move on, and my companions, the Tuaregs are all ready, kitted up and have made preparations for the next stage of the journey. The camels are watered, supplies are on board, and I get back on my donkey still looking incongruous. Calmly, quietly, and with no haste, we set off once more across the land.

They tell me, "When you travel across places that are not peopled, you are able to draw on your own thoughts. You can think in an uncluttered way with no distractions. When you reach your destination, your mind will have a new understanding, a new awareness of the priorities of things, of the order and of perspective. One is able to see the plan in all its facets."

The leader of the three turns round and looks at me in a different way, and it's—how can I say — looking to make sure I am all right? . . . I can't quite get that wording. Instead of trailing behind them as usual, the one in the lead and ones on either side have altered their pace so that my donkey has come up in between. Instead of me having to trail behind, I'm in between and closer to them and more protected. I feel the emotion of that, and my chest hurts. It ends and I return home.

2. Three Tuaregs—a blessing

I go through doors and find myself on a long path. I walk between old men, all sitting on the ground cross-legged, smiling and nodding at me. I wave as I go. They do not attempt to stop me, for they're not the ones I've come to see. They are sitting on either side of the path. This trail seems to go on forever, out into what appears to be hot desert. It is not isolated, just desert, sandy Middle Eastern country. I keep walking. I do not know where I'm going. I see a donkey, more than one donkey. I walk along with the donkeys. Some of them are laden, and some of them are not. I still do not know where I'm going.

Then I see my Tuaregs, which takes me by surprise because I did not expect to see them. They are facing the same direction as me. That is interesting because they usually come towards me. They are not on camels. They are on horses, walking at a snail's pace. I can catch them up easily. I do not think they have seen me. The horses are stepping very slowly. I am alongside them now and am having to walk quite fast even though they are not moving quickly. I do not know whether to let them know I am here or not. I keep pace with them. Suddenly they speed up and wheel round so that they are blocking my path and facing me. The donkeys have stopped as well, for they are not used to being blocked by horses and men in this way. The donkeys swarm around me as I stand still.

The Tuaregs dismount, all of them. They hold their horses by the bridle, holding them still, because of all the donkeys milling around. The middle one comes towards me. I still have never been able to see his face. I see only his very dark eyes. He comes close and stands in front of me. I look and feel very small. He takes my hands and puts them together. I do not know what he's going to do with them. He puts them together and presses them to his forehead. His hands are around mine. When he has touched his brow, he puts them towards mine. I don't know if this is a greeting or what. He lets them go, and I stand there wondering what to do next. He beckons me to go with him. Not a word has been spoken.

He walks on, holding his horse; I walk alongside him. We are spread out across the road. The donkeys are following. I have absolutely no idea what this means. There is nothing in front of us. All the old men are still sitting on either side of the road, nodding and waving. It feels like a procession, and I feel a bit stupid. We are going to meet somebody. They are taking me to meet somebody. We come to a big wall and go through an opening. We file through, the donkeys follow as well.

There is an old man sitting under a tree, waiting. We go up to him as he stands up. He is quite tall and is very special. He looks extremely calm and very gentle. He puts his hand out and places it on my head. I feel blessed. I have come here to be blessed. Though this man is not dressed in anything splendid, I know he is splendid. I know he is a superb being. I almost feel as if he is not there, is not real, is not solid, and might almost disappear at any time. I am looking at a spirit with the body placed around it so that I can see it. It is not really there. I feel very faint and dizzy as if I too might not be there at any moment, as if I too might disappear. Silence as I return to my world.

3. The Three Tuaregs—on Equal Footing

Three Tuaregs come up and are in front of me. They are on camels, high up and looking down at me. I stand before them. I am a woman wrapped up in desert clothes. All of them dismount. They are still very tall compared to me. They walk and surround me so that I have one on either side and one in front. I can only see their eyes. The middle one looks directly into my eyes and takes in my whole form with his glance. I do not feel uncomfortable as I stand there. We remain silent. He gets down on his knees, and I do the same. We both kneel on the sand and extend our arms to hold hands. With hands joined, we bow forward so that our heads are resting on the ground. We are joined in a form of greeting, but it is not a greeting just to each other, it is a greeting for something much greater, an acknowledgment of something greater. My head is covered.

Leaning back on our heels, we release hands. He helps me up. I look around for the usual donkey that they have for me. But there isn't any donkey. There is nothing but these three men. They don't get back on their camels but all walk forward together. I am in the middle. We are in a line and walk forward like a vanguard.

I do not know where we're going. We are literally on equal footing, for we are all walking on the same sand, the same ground, one not more in front than the other. We are in line, equal status, equal footing and on the same journey. The fact that I do not know where we are going does not matter. I assume they do know. It is warming to the heart, very safe and secure. There is enormous feeling of companionship. I'm very much one of them now. We are not separated by time, distance, or status. We are equal on all counts.

We keep on walking. There must be a destination, surely. We are coming up to a low set of buildings. As we arrive on the outskirts of these buildings, people come out to greet us. We are travelers, we have traveled far and know we will be fed and welcomed into people's hearts. We are taken in, given accommodation and food. But our duty does not end there. They expect something from us. I have to talk and tell them of the experiences along the way, to tell them what I've learned along the way.

My companions are Guardians of the Way. It is they who have brought me here so that I can play my part. My part is to speak to the peoples and tell them about life and death and the continuation of everything. I'm to explain to them the passage that they must walk through. To explain that what they meet on their journey can only assist them, that these things have been in place even before their arrival, waiting to be set in motion for their benefit.

They listen and react, according to their own hearts. We have been welcomed, sheltered, and cared for. Before we continue our way, part of our stay is to look at the sick and to do what we can. It is an expected part of our visit. We would not be fulfilling our role if we did not include this. We would not be completing our mission if we ignored this.

My life continued in what many would call a normal existence with visits to friends and family, shopping, cleaning, and all things that make a life normal. I continued to run workshops, give readings and the occasional lecture. Hidden from that life was another world, only shared when I did a channelling. On the surface my family knew of my activities, especially my overseas visits for my work, but they did not delve too deeply. They have never asked any questions, preferring to keep on safe ground. My adult children have even bought my published books and my eldest son manages my website. However they have no idea of my other worlds Would I ever be able to be open about my journeys to other realms? I doubted it and had to consider that my darling much-loved family would never ever understand.

Chapter 28

Speak Out

> Those who have the courage to stand up and speak what is in their heart often reach the hearts of others and give an opening for expression that might otherwise have remained hidden. Never be fearful of making a fool of oneself, for courage is admired and not ridiculed. May wisdom guide your words.
>
> *From the Little Owl Cards*

On my return, I had a dream. In it I saw Andreas hurrying to meet up with a group of influential men. I had never seen him hurry before. They were all grouped together, heads huddled over something in the middle of their circle. I craned my neck to see what it was and found it was a globe, the planet Earth. To my horror, I could see it turning black where it had previously been blue and green. I saw them sticking tiny colored patches all over it and was reminded of flags stuck in a wall map as markers.

Andreas left them to their work and walked over to another group, which I saw was comprised of Dr.Po, Raman the Rajah, and even the Tuaregs. I went in closer, hoping to hear some of their conversation.

"We have to do something," Andreas was saying. "They are confused and do not know what to do."

"Leave it to us," the others said. It was strange that they didn't appear to know I was there. I reminded myself that it was only a dream after all. Odd that I knew it was a dream while still in it. To my disgust, I woke up. What did it all mean? What had they in mind this time?

Was I the one who was confused? I decided not to wait to find out, but to ask. I determined that during meditation that morning I would ask for an explanation. I did not have to wait long. Rather it was as if they'd been waiting for me.

The slight form of Dr.Po in his long, heavily brocaded coat appeared before me. He bowed, his dour face giving nothing away. "Good morning, little one. Did you have a good night?" I detected a trace of humor and amusement in his voice.

"We have come to give you preparation, to prepare the mind and the heart. We come to demonstrate what is required. Those who wish to find happiness and those who wish to find peace and contentment forevermore would do well to take note of what we have to say. It is time to brush off the dust and to renew the values that have been taught in previous times, which have been ignored by so many.

"We ask that you conduct your life to the best of your abilities, to the level that you are capable of reaching. We do not ask for more. You will be encouraged to reach a wider understanding and strength so that when you are ready, you will make a greater sacrifice of self.

"We ask that you provide proof that there are space friends in other existences working in harmony with you, attempting to assist by all means at their disposal through the energy fields. We are attempting to communicate with all those who are able to receive. Those who do receive have a responsibility placed upon them, to spread the content of that which they have been given, not to hold it in. We ask that you open your mouth and speak what you feel in your heart. You will find there are many like you. It needs but one to begin, so that others in their turn will open and share their experiences, their communications, whether it is communication through meditation, in the dream state, or by flashes of inspiration.

"Thought transference is more widespread than you believe. You are aware that thoughts have a vibration and that thoughts can transcend time, space, and physical matter. In short, thoughts can reach their target. Words too have a vibration. Words have the benefit of being heard on a physical level by those who are not fine-tuned to vibration of thought. Words, once heard, cannot be forgotten. Everything that is seen, heard, or felt is retained within the memory and is never lost.

"We are assuming that most of mankind desires peace and contentment and happiness, even if for selfish reasons. It is a natural desire. We are merely asking that you show as many as possible how to achieve a state of happiness. Again I can feel you saying, there is much misery in the world, much cruelty, and this is true. Do not consider your task to be impossibly large, for if you take that line of thought, you will be beaten before you begin.

"You are not alone in your endeavors. As you know, there is a team of us who direct operations and influence the minds that are ready and open. We influence those who are not afraid to be in the front line to open the lines of communication for all, for that is what is required. If you have been observant, you will note that this is already happening in many areas despite opposition. Are you aware that there is opposition?"

I shook my head. He paused. "Opposition? From where?" I asked.

"Do you not remember we spoke earlier of powerful energies from those who do not follow our way of thinking or endeavor?"

I remembered.

"Who do you think is responsible for enabling violence to be shown on your screens, influencing so many young and not-so-young minds? Remember that anything once seen, once heard is never forgotten in the mind, even by those who find the subject matter distasteful. Have you never viewed something horrific and turned away, only to find that the image remains with you in spite of yourself? And too, that this same image returned in unguarded moments. You then feel uneasy with yourself for having fastened onto something you do not wish to be a part of you. You guiltily ask, what is wrong with you that this lives in you, in spite of yourself? You know that there is an attraction as well as revulsion. What is happening here is that these images strike a chord of recognition from the memory of past lives. Maybe many, many lives ago."

I shuddered as I thought of the public hangings and Roman theaters where Christians were torn apart by wild animals to the delight of watching crowds.

Dr.Po stared hard at me. "Everything that has ever happened to you in your soul's journey is never forgotten or lost. How you react and deal with these disturbing awakenings within is dependent on the power and strength of your own mind energies. Are you able to let these images go, having once dealt with them in former times? So many cannot dismiss what they have seen from their minds, dwelling upon the horror of what they have seen and allowing the force of recognition to grow in strength until it dominates their thoughts and actions to the detriment of their being.

"The past cannot be eliminated, but you can ensure that history does not repeat itself over and over again. You can ensure that that which has been conquered and overcome in the past does not need to actively re-emerge. Do not feel guilty but accept that this has been part of you and has been dealt with."

He paused again, his sad eyes searching my face to see if I was taking this all in. I felt he was trying to say we humans could reverse the tide of cruelty and counteract the influence of the opposition. I understood him so far, but it was a lot to absorb all at once. The sweet perfume about him wafted over me. I felt this too was intentional, and my mind began to focus more sharply. His mind was ahead of mine, as always.

"Those of you who deplore the destructive influence on your screens have it in their power to eliminate it. One does not need to have abilities of a special nature to do this. Each individual upon the planet is able to act, if they are so minded.

"The producers of any program on your screens, whether this be television or cinema, will say that they supply what the public demands. That, after all, is the quickest way to make profit, and one cannot blame them for this. You are the public, yes?"

"Yes," I agreed.

"You and many others like you deplore and lament on the quality and harmful influence of some programs and yet do nothing but grumble among yourselves. If sufficient numbers of the public were to write to the producers and the suppliers of unsavory material, then quite obviously, notice would be taken. They would supply only what the public demanded. It is not in their interests to do otherwise. So it is up to you all. This is just one way. You have the means and the power to oppose negative and harmful influences in your world."

"I see what you mean," I said thoughtfully. "But what has all this to do with the dreadful scenes shown in the viewing room? I assume these events are set to happen?"

"What we are concerned with is the preparation of the peoples of the world for events to come. We are not speaking so much about practical readiness but rather about understanding.

"Do you remember how earlier we compared the Earth to a sick patient requiring drastic surgery, as a result of past neglect? She is finding it difficult to breathe (the air). Her blood is poisoned (the waters). The flesh (the earth) has been gouged, scarred, burnt, and abused until it can no longer rejuvenate itself. What is more, the microbes (plant and animal life) that feed, enrich, and protect her have also become contaminated, so they too diminish."

He continued with the comparison, "Surgeons think they can save her and are making preparation for the operation or series of operations that are necessary for this. However, as you are aware, the negative or positive attitude and conditions surrounding any patient has a great deal to do with recovery. Any good medical team makes sure beforehand that the patient is strong enough to pull through. All conditions surrounding the patient should be as positive as possible." Dr.Po, the dear old man, quivered with deep emotion. I felt a great need to comfort him.

"Is this where mankind has a part to play?" I asked tenderly. I wanted to put my arms round his bony shoulders. His face was full of anxiety. The planet clearly meant a great deal to him, even though he no longer needed it himself.

As if remembering his part, he smiled weakly. "Oh, little one, if only men knew that they could do so much to save themselves and their world. Constant striving for improvement in the air, waters, and land is required to ensure recovery of Mother Earth after the operation. What is not required is continual abuse which further weakens an already weak state." He looked sadly at me and placed a bony hand on mine.

"I will leave now. We will be in communication again shortly. Do not be concerned, little one."

It was he who looked concerned, I thought to myself, as he left me to ponder over all that had passed between us. Was the situation really so grave that even this learned teacher was saddened, or was that just his nature?

Chapter 29

New ways of communicating

The years move on swiftly with so much happening all over the world that it is hard to keep up. Is it just me or do others feel it is more than we can handle?

A time thief has crept into my world. It is a blessing and a curse at the same time.

I remember when there was no internet, no personal computers, no mobile phones, no instant access to whatever we wanted. I achieved much more then than now as I was not side-tracked. Is the internet a NET in other senses of the word?

I continue to meditate but not as often as before. When I do and ask the right questions I get answers. Fortunately my spirit friends have not deserted me and when I link in their energy pulses through me just as powerfully. I am happily relieved that I have not *lost* my connection during all the upheavals of what is happening in the world today.

The questions come from other avenues, from other people. The answers are still from spirit. I am requested to ask questions of spirit by those I have not seen or met. This can be through the wonderful digital means of Zoom meetings or emails. It is no bad thing for it keeps us united without having to travel. One such question was put during a Zoom presentation. The timing was perfect for it coincided with a message that came a little earlier about Earth Changes.

Jan 14th 2003 Channelled by me

"The Earth is one cell of a giant body, a giant everything. Cells can divide."

I have a picture of the Earth splitting into two in the way a cell divides. I have just got the word 'cloning'. The Angelic Force is coming in.

"We are to do this, rather differently if we can, for purposes of illustration. As to the future, The Angelic Force and those who would protect, oversee and guide evolution of the Creation, not simply the planet Earth but all of Creation. The Force and the guidance that this it is able to produce can indeed materialise a completely new cosmic body, in form relative to the Creation that can appear, can seem miraculous and relatively instantaneous. However if you think of time then this is protracted. We do not think in Earth time and we know, for it has been decided, that a new cosmic body be produced for the benefit of humankind. So indeed, in your words, it could be called a cloning."

Questioner: Has this been done before?

"It has. You might call yourselves experimental. You might even call yourselves a prototype, for we are modifying, improving and producing yet better models as time goes on. We find it difficult to put into your language. It has been done before and no doubt it will be done again in the future."

Questioner: Souls who take part in this experiment, do they agree to do this?

"They agree as they progress. There isn't agreement in total by all souls at one time. As their own lives renew, or die if they are physical, they are faced with choices. The choices are put before them and they may agree, or they may not. Each soul will progress according to its choice. So, yes there is agreement for those who wish to follow the Earth's progression. Nobody is forced into anything. Gravity will reassert itself."

Zoom questioner. August 1st 2020

Q: When will we transition to the new Earth and how will this happen? Please elaborate.

Response from spirit: "It is quite clear. Think of the new Earth as a birth. Transition is very similar to the gestation of a child through its mother, attached to its mother by the umbilical cord within the womb. The new Earth is going through this process within the womb of your current Earth and attached to it. As the movement and growth develops, as it does with all new things, this is fed by the mother and grows accordingly. The question was when will the transition take place?

"The time comes for the birth and the New Earth comes through still attached to the umbilical cord for a while. Within that umbilical cord and while it is being developed, DNA and all sorts of influences pass along to the new Birth. Once it has passed on to the New, it is there, not to be removed. And so the New Earth emerges and grows and the umbilical cord is severed. The New Earth has the DNA of the old Earth.

"Remember this is an analogy only. There are aspects, genetics passed from the mother to the new being. Some are not transferred and are left behind and yet others, as in all new ones, some genes are carried forward and some are not. It is the same thing. Each gene, each characteristic needs to be in tune, comfortable, vibrate happily with its new form, otherwise it does not pass through, it simply remains with its original mother.

"So, separation takes place and the New Earth, the New Being vibrates as all new things do with life, vitality and the urge to learn, discover and grow. It is as with all new things which are not yet a mature being. It will search, learn, and grasp as it goes along. It will be in a state of growth for a considerable amount of time, as it was with the Old Earth.

"You have asked 'when'. The process has begun already with

the conception (*in the mind?)* of the New Earth at the beginning and it takes time for the development. And we know you are saying that this does not tell us when. We are telling you that it has already happened. The New Earth is there ready and waiting to learn, to grow and for all the DNA, genetics to grow, beginning, learning. As with all new things there will be those who take care of it so it is not alone and will be monitored. It will be watched over, it will be tended and made sure that only good things happen to this New Earth. The dangers are kept at bay. To answer the question, it has already happened but is in its new stage.

"Now you are thinking of individuals, yourself perhaps. How does it feel? Will you know?

"You are already incorporated as – shall we call you a DNA, a cell, part of the new Being? Integral, not to be separated for ever until that Earth too passes on in its time. You are already there, you become aware with the growth. As we said, the New Earth will become aware of all things new. It will learn, it will discover, it will feel its way. You as part of this will go along with it and learn to develop as well. This is as much as we need to tell you at this time."

I find it is very important when you have the opportunity to ask questions during any Zoom presentations, send in the questions in advance so giving the one who channels time to ask spirit beforehand.

Chapter 30

In My Suitcase

Many times my friends say, "Please take me in your suitcase." Or, aren't you lucky, traveling all over to unusual places. Can't you take me with you?"

I would say to them, if you want to travel, buy the ticket The way I go is not to everybody's taste and is not in luxury. I rarely stay in hotels since I do not have the money for that. I go where I am invited and am fed and accommodated for the work I do. Although most of the places I stay in are comfortable and clean, some are not. Here are some examples of what I mean, though I will not give countries or names in case I offend. I have frequently accepted an offer without knowing the hosts or their habits beforehand.

I travel alone since it is easier for hosts to accommodate a single person than two.

Expectations of what I can do varies tremendously. I try to give clear guidelines in advance as to how many readings I can do in one day, but often, when I arrive I find that I am booked to do seven hours of readings during the day and then channel soul readings for the entire evening, and give a talk and do a workshop at the weekend. I do not mind since that is what I am there for. This goes on for two weeks in each venue before I go on to the next. I usually manage it so as not to disappoint but am quite tired and ready to go home at the end of my stay. Also, if you want to be invited back, you know you must be able to meet everybody's expectations in a satisfactory way.

These are some uncomfortable examples from a variety of countries.

I arrived, hot and sticky after a very long flight. I was shown the room where I was to sleep. It was untidy but was acceptable. What was not acceptable was when I put my feet onto the floor when getting out of bed next morning and to step onto dog poo that had clearly been there for quite a while. The rest of the house was filthy with flies everywhere. I thought the carpet in the main room was patterned with dots until on closer inspection I saw they were cigarette burns. The good side was that I met a great many wonderful people who came for the workshops or readings. I felt blessed to have met them. Sometimes you have to take the good with the not so good, but I will not go there again.

Another place was so bad that I telephoned a friend and asked to be rescued. This house was piled so high with rubbish in every corner that to get to my bed I had to climb over large black plastic bags stuffed full of goodness knows what. There was not a space to be found to even put a cup down, and I am not exaggerating. My host did not get up till midday even though I had readings booked throughout the day, with nowhere suitable to do them.

Yet another venue was miles from any shops and had no public transport, but with no food in the house.

"I'm slimming," my host explained, "and I only eat Slim-Fast. I don't cook." I was saved from hunger by a neighbor who took me in to town to buy supplies and who occasionally fed me. Several days, the only food I had all day were a couple of bread rolls. This kind Samaritan I have since visited in her in Texas and she is still my friend today.

It was in the same country that I had proof that my spirit friends had organised it all. Before leaving UK I was told in a meditation to take my Crystal Sword with me. On my fist day I went to sit on the beach and relax after my long flight. Suddenly a native of that country came out of the sea and approached me quite purposefully.

"Oh, it is you," he said.

Surprised I looked at him and asked." What do you mean?"

"They told me to look for the white-haired lady with the crystal sword."

He proceeded to tell me all about the cosmic cousins and spoke their language and showed me their writing. During my stay we later continued our discussion and after a difficult climb up through cacti to a cave he said was special I gave him my very first Soul Reading.

Yet another country my stay venue was clean and tidy, and I was fed well. However, on getting into bed, I felt something at the bottom of the sheets. Investigating, I pulled out two pairs of men's dirty underpants. Clearly the sheets had not been changed for my stay.

Sometimes it is the atmosphere between two people that makes it uncomfortable. One place I went to, the couple were so antagonistic to each other that I was caught in the middle as each on separate occasions they told me their side of things. In this case, I had the added strain of trying to eat my food without their two dogs getting to the plate first. I ate with my arm around the dish while pushing the animals off with the other arm.

"Don't leave anything on the table or chairs," I was warned. "The dogs will get it." They were right. I watched as food was prepared and the dogs' wet muzzles slopped all over it before it went into the pot. And they wondered why I did not repeat the experience when invited back!

It was quite normal in some places, such as Australia, to be brought a swag roll and to bed down on the floor of the room where I was to hold a workshop. This was surprisingly comfortable, but now I am in my late eighties, I do not wish to continue in this way.

The challenging experiences are not always down to unthinking hosts, but to the climate and country. On one occasion, I was again in northern Brazil far from towns or civilization. One memorable experience was during the wet season when the water table had risen. I awoke one night to feel the mattress moving under me. I was rolled back and forth as I lay there for a while wondering what it could be. Thoughts of snakes went through my mind. I knew they had big ones. It was dark, so I decided to switch on my torch and tuck my mosquito net more firmly under the mattress. Nothing could get in that way, I thought. As I looked over the edge, I saw many eyes staring back at me, as surprised as I was. Was it a mouse or a rat? I could not decide. There was nothing I could do about that. At least it wasn't a snake after all. I went back to sleep. Next morning I discovered that my watch had been dragged into the shower room and the leather strap chewed. I was only glad I hadn't been wearing the watch. It was clear from investigation next morning that mice or rats were nesting in the mattress.

Do you still want to come with me? You would be most welcome.

Generally, I am looked after well and have comfortable accommodation, but there are exceptions. I think I have experienced them all.

In meditation I think twice now before asking spirit where they want me to be because they will tell me, and I will go even though my age makes it less easy.

These days I am drawn to attend conferences where like-minded people gather and where I learn so much more. I also have the luxury of staying in a hotel. I have had the enormous pleasure of meeting amazing people such as Edgar Mitchell, the 6th man to walk on the moon.

Then there was John Mack who signed his book for me. I had the privilege of hearing Jaime Maussan give his presentation on our cosmic cousins being here on our Earth and also surrounding our planet. Being in the company of these people is comforting in that I am not deluding myself in my interactions with our cosmic friends. They all speak with great authority when demonstrating that none of us are alone.

Many connections I have made at these conferences have led

me to work and visit such places as Alaska and all over Australia. There is the bonus that I stay in hotels at these conferences. I continue to do what the spirit friends have asked of me. I share what I have discovered without worrying about ridicule. I teach how to contact wonderful beings. So many discover that they can indeed do this for themselves, and as a result, their lives have changed for the better. New worlds open for them with a feeling of peace and calm resolution to be the best they can.

Chapter 31

We Are One as We Journey

May you always hold kindness in your soul,
Compassion in your heart,
Gentleness in your actions,
Truth in your words,
And wisdom in your thoughts,
so that you may be effective
and as a shining light wherever you tread.
May the effect of your touch be comforting,
and a healing to those who have a need.
May you hold goodness of all life in your Being.
Then your journey through life will have been
worthwhile.

ET Osishoo

Are We Worth Saving?

As we view the world about us and see the terrible things human beings do to other human beings and other living creatures, we can be forgiven for thinking that we as a species are on a slippery slope. We could alternatively remind ourselves that we have come a long way. So many of us have the ability, conscience, and compassion towards our fellow humans to do something about our state. We could ask, are there interplanetary beings and angels living among us? Are we already becoming greater human beings? What is happening today, and what is to happen on and around the Earth very soon? Are those events mentioned earlier to be welcomed, ignored, or feared? What is our connection to the stars? Who were the gods of ancient legends? Answers to these questions are coming thick and fast, not only through spirit communication but also through scientific discoveries. How we prepare ourselves for a stupendous leap in evolution for mankind is of importance to our future.

Most are aware of the other dimension we go to when we die. We are currently in the third dimension and moving forward. This fact is no surprise to anyone, even to those who do not think about these things. We have a long way to go. The good news is that it gets better as we climb to those dizzy heights. Even one step is a vast improvement on our present status as human beings.

Many on this Earth have experienced the lower levels of the fourth dimension, through near-death experiences or during altered states of awareness in meditation. They say how wonderful that world is and how they wished they could have stayed. Have any of us been in the fourth dimension before or even into higher realms? Of course we have. Between physical lives our soul consciousness is free and is able to travel where it will, according to its level of vibration. Knowingly or unknowingly, we can go there during our sleep state or during meditation. We speak of light beings and light-workers, both in physical and nonphysical form. What is important is that we shed our light into the dark and help others on their way, no matter who we think we are.

We are told that there is no such thing as time, and yet we feel we are bound by time. We rush here and there, trying to get everything done in time for this or that. However, when we meditate, even for only five minutes, we find that our inner journeys cover vast tracks of events. Time loses meaning. We can access the past, present, or future with ease. We can visit other planets or enter free space. Do we believe what we experience? Even as a creation of our imagination, it is a reality and so it exists. We can *image create* worlds of wonder, health and happiness. These worlds exist and can be entered, for they have been imaged before and have not disappeared from reality. Are these then the other dimensions?

We have been there before if you believe there is no such thing as time. Many on Earth now are truly interdimensional beings. I have spoken to entities when channeling who affirm this. Our own mythology speaks of giants, gods, fairies, mythical creatures, and other great beings that inhabited the Earth. They speak of Atlantis and the great powers of those who lived at that time. Where do these stories come from, if not from reality?

I believe that many of you here now, teachers, healers, walk-ins, incarnated angels, old souls or new, and reincarnating Atlanteans have come as a new, immense spiritual wave sent to Earth, to assist those who do not understand that we are about to enter a greater dimension in a lighter, less dense physical form. We come from many planets and have been here for a very long time, to understand the nature of our role and of all aspects of humanity. The White Brotherhood tells me that there is to be a new root race of man, that mankind is leaving behind the Adamic period and entering a new level of being. We are making a leap up in our evolution irrespective of the misguided minority areas of society.

Already I am meeting many who have a wide comprehension of the nature of our existence, who show great knowledge and spiritual understanding. Many clients who come to me for channeled soul readings discover they are from other worlds, are teachers, have come from a higher realm. I am delighted to inform my visitors of their mission and heritage. They usually go on to achieve astounding things as a result. All any of us need is encouragement and inspiration. There is a great awakening on this Earth.

I and others like me are already speaking in a language not of this Earth, where the vibrations of the sounds have a healing effect. The latest development is the training by our space visitors to understand telepathically the languages they give us in sound. My little group is told that we will be the interpreters for those who cannot receive telepathically when the visitors from other worlds make themselves physically present and when they wish to use their own language, which is useful for changing energies and healing.

You can also help the Earth itself. She has suffered greatly through the activities of mankind. You all have an energetic field that surrounds us that we call the aura or etheric body, and you may go to healers or therapists to assist you when your field is ragged. Earth too has a magnetic, energy field, a life force that needs to be in good shape for her rebirth. Those of you who work with Earth energies can listen to your guidance and travel in your minds or physically, to where the Earth energies need reinforcing.

You are infinite souls and cannot be erased from existence. Where you go is dependent on the quality of your light, your souls. You grow according to your behavior, which truly reflects the quality of your being. In the world to come, you will be seen for what you are, lighter bodies. There will be no hiding place for lies or false power. You are urged to focus on your soul and its journey.

If you have ever seen your planet from afar, you will have been astounded and moved by the beauty and wonder of it. Most of us have seen satellite or space shots of our glorious home which we call Earth.

Go in a little closer, and it becomes even more amazing with its variety of climates and terrains. Zoom in even more, and you begin to see scarring and pollution, even in the oceans. But zoom in even more closely, and you will see in the darkest places acts of shining example, acts of enormous sacrifice within families and society, acts of courage under pain, acts of selflessness in giving up time to make another's life better. There are acts of caring for those unable to help themselves, acts of kindness towards those less well endowed, either physically or mentally. Everywhere in the harshest conditions, the human being demonstrates endurance, patience, and bravery. All over the planet are shining examples of extreme bravery, of loving acts, of care for others and resistance to tyranny and oppression.

All over the planet, the human being has demonstrated to ability to make discoveries, to seek for more and more knowledge, and to strive for improvement in living conditions and better moral standards. Everywhere in the most unlikely places there are people who strive to understand their reason for being. Everywhere are people who find the time to pray together for the benefit of another, whom they might not even know. Humanity has proved that it can adapt to whatever circumstances it finds itself in. It has already done this successfully over the ages.

Wherever we think we may have come from or whatever our origins, it is certain that we are all here to experience what it is to be a human. It is a privilege to be human and have all the emotions that go with that. Can you imagine a world without feeling love, joy, delight, laughter, and enthusiasm? There are many worlds where they are striving to get back to those feelings, so they might grow and stay connected to spirit.

Are we worth saving? The answer is a resounding *yes*. For as long as you and others continue to amaze the celestial beings and intelligent species on other planetary systems, for as long as you shine as beacons in dark places, this planet we call Earth will receive all the help and support it desperately needs from them and our space friends. Yes, we are worth saving.

Collectively we are now ready to step up into the higher dimensions that are being spoken of and at times are experiencing. Great souls will arise during this time of disarray. Great souls will surpass all others, and those who wish to be great can look to them and receive inspiration in the sight. All will surpass and outweigh the evils that are occurring on your planet. Things will go well. Your soul has the opportunity to rise and not fall. God bless you all.

It is a great time to be alive. May your own journeys be as wonderful and uplifting as mine still are today.

IS IT THE END OR THE BEGINNING?

LOVE EVERY PERSON YOU COME INTO CONTACT WITH.
LOVE OPENS A CHANNEL FOR THE DIVINE.
HATE OPENS A CHANNEL FOR EVIL

Acknowledgments and Thanks

In no particular order:

My thanks to Roy Breeze who got me started on my journey. Without him, I might never have got off the ground, in more ways than one.

Thanks to Karynne Ledger for her wonderful and accurate drawings of my guides. See www.ledgerstudio.com.

My thanks to Pat Law who gave me the opportunity to give my very first talk in public. I still remember those shaking knees.

Thanks to all those who have not said I am wasting my time.

Thanks to my spirit friends and star people for their love and patience.

Thanks to those mediums and psychics who have pointed the way and encouraged me to continue when I doubted myself.

Thanks to Doris Stokes, who in spirit stood by my side on the platform in Washington DC.

So many thanks to the White Brotherhood who have given me such insight and so many beautiful and profound words for the Little Owl Cards. They are a treasure.

Dear readers, if you have enjoyed this book and my other books please leave a review on Amazon and let me know.

www.littleowlonline.co.uk shirleymbattie@gmail.com

Printed in Great Britain
by Amazon

83167453R00173